This Book
Belongs To:

_____

LIBRARY *of* CLASSIC POETS

W. B. Yeats

Selected Poems

W. B. Yeats

Selected Poems

Gramercy Books
New York

This 2001 edition is published by Gramercy Books™,
an imprint of Random House Value Publishing, Inc.,
280 Park Avenue, New York, New York 10017.

Gramercy Books™ and design are trademarks of Random House Value Publishing, Inc.

Random House
New York • Toronto • London • Sydney • Auckland
http://www.randomhouse.com/

Printed and bound in the United States of America

Library of Congress Cataloging-in-Publication Data
Yeats. W. B. (William Butler), 1865-1939.
[Poems. Selections]
Selected poems of William Butler Yeats.—1991 ed.
p. cm.
ISBN 0-517-07396-X
I. Title
PR5902   1991
821'.8—dc20   91-39166   CIP

16 15 14 13 12 11

CONTENTS

The Wind Among the Reeds

In the Seven Woods

The Old Age of Queen Maeve

Baile and Aillinn

The Green Helmet and Other Poems

Responsibilities

Responsibilities

INTRODUCTION

William Butler Yeats is an Irish poet, not an English poet. It is an important distinction which Yeats throughout his career made clear. Although the Yeats family was of English descent, by the time of William's birth—in Dublin on June 13, 1865—they had been in Ireland for more than two hundred years. Yeats grew up in a turbulent era of increasing Irish nationalism and rebellion against English rule and he became actively involved in the struggle for Irish independence. By the early 1890s he had helped form the Irish Literary Society of London and the National Literary Society in Dublin to promote Irish cultural awareness. In 1896, he became a member of the Irish Republican Brotherhood, an organization which actively sought independence, by violent means if necessary. In 1922, to reward his patriotic efforts, he was made a senator in the newly formed Irish Free State. But his real contribution to Ireland was literary: In 1923 he became the first Irishman to win the Nobel Prize in literature.

Yeats believed that political and economic independence for Ireland was not sufficient, and that equally or more important was freedom from England's materialistic culture. He felt that the richness and vitality of the more pastoral Irish way of life were reflected in its myths, legends, and folklore and believed that through the cultivation of its art Ireland could revive its unique culture and "preserve an ancient ideal of life." Yeats became a leader in the movement known as the Irish Literary Renaissance. One of their major projects was the establishment in 1904 of the Irish National Theatre (later the Abbey Theatre), a showcase for talented Irish playwrights, including Yeats, Sean O'Casey, and John Synge.

But Yeats's greatest contribution to the movement was his own poetry. He is Ireland's greatest poet and many believe that no other modern English or American poet can match his vision and versatility. This book is a collection of poems from the first half of his career. The poems trace his development from a talented late-Romantic poet into one of the most powerful and unique voices of twentieth-century verse.

Through all the changes in the style and substance of Yeats's poetry there is one constant—the musical quality of his language. For him poetry and music were inseparable. He believed poetry arises from the magic spells of ancient and mystical sorcerers. His poems are always pleasing to the ear, and this is his most powerful hold over the reader, perhaps explaining his popularity not only with critics but also with the general reader, who may not always understand the complex symbolism contained in his poetry. Yeats's genius and ultimate craft lay in his realization of this. As he himself said, "I like a poem to have fine machinery, but if [it] is made to appear anything more than that, the spell of the poetry is broken." Yeats died on January 28, 1939. He was certainly the most successful magician of his age.

CHRISTOPHER MOORE

New York
1992

Early Poems

— I —

BALLADS AND LYRICS

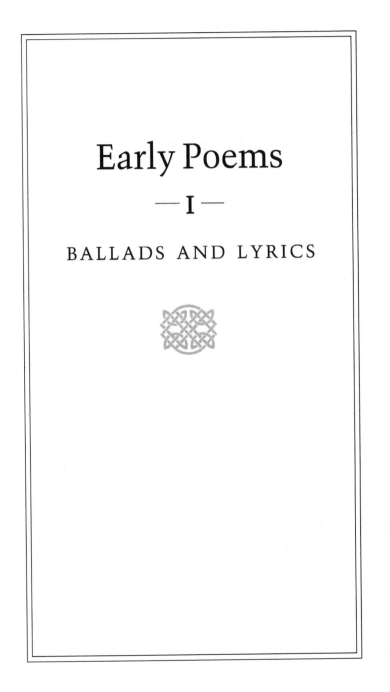

"The stars are threshed, and the souls are threshed from their husks."

WILLIAM BLAKE

TO SOME I HAVE TALKED WITH
BY THE FIRE. A DEDICATION TO
A VOLUME OF EARLY POEMS

While I wrought out these fitful Danaan rhymes,
My heart would brim with dreams about the times
When we bent down above the fading coals;
And talked of the dark folk, who live in souls
Of passionate men, like bats in the dead trees;
And of the wayward twilight companies,
Who sigh with mingled sorrow and content,
Because their blossoming dreams have never bent
Under the fruit of evil and of good;
And of the embattled flaming multitude
Who rise, wing above wing, flame above flame,
And, like a storm, cry the Ineffable Name;
And with the clashing of their sword blades make
A rapturous music, till the morning break,
And the white hush end all, but the loud beat
Of their long wings, the flash of their white feet.

THE SONG OF THE HAPPY SHEPHERD

The woods of Arcady are dead,
And over is their antique joy;
Of old the world on dreaming fed;
Gray Truth is now her painted toy;
Yet still she turns her restless head:
But O, sick children of the world,
Of all the many changing things
In dreary dancing past us whirled,
To the cracked tune that Chronos sings,
Words alone are certain good.
Where are now the warring kings,
Word be-mockers?—By the Rood
Where are now the warring kings?
An idle word is now their glory,
By the stammering schoolboy said,
Reading some entangled story:
The kings of the old time are fled.
The wandering earth herself may be
Only a sudden flaming word,
In clanging space a moment heard,
Troubling the endless reverie.

Then no wise worship dusty deeds,
Nor seek; for this is also sooth;
To hunger fiercely after truth,
Lest all thy toiling only breeds
New dreams, new dreams; there is no
    truth
Saving in thine own heart. Seek, then,
No learning from the starry men,
Who follow with the optic glass
The whirling ways of stars that pass—

Seek, then, for this is also sooth,
No word of theirs—the cold star-bane
Has cloven and rent their hearts in
        twain,
And dead is all their human truth.
Go gather by the humming sea
Some twisted, echo-harbouring shell,
And to its lips thy story tell,
And they thy comforters will be,
Rewording in melodious guile,
Thy fretful words a little while,
Till they shall singing fade in ruth,
And die a pearly brotherhood;
For words alone are certain good:
Sing, then, for this is also sooth.

I must be gone: there is a grave
Where daffodil and lily wave,
And I would please the hapless faun,
Buried under the sleepy ground,
With mirthful songs before the dawn.
His shouting days with mirth were crowned;
And still I dream he treads the lawn,
Walking ghostly in the dew,
Pierced by my glad singing through,
My songs of old earth's dreamy youth:
But ah! she dreams not now; dream thou!
For fair are poppies on the brow:
Dream, dream, for this is also sooth.

THE SAD SHEPHERD

There was a man whom Sorrow named his friend,
And he, of his high comrade Sorrow dreaming,
Went walking with slow steps along the gleaming
And humming sands, where windy surges wend:
And he called loudly to the stars to bend
From their pale thrones and comfort him, but they
Among themselves laugh on and sing alway:
And then the man whom Sorrow named his friend
Cried out, *Dim sea, hear my most piteous story!*
The sea swept on and cried her old cry still,
Rolling along in dreams from hill to hill;
He fled the persecution of her glory
And, in a far-off, gentle valley stopping,
Cried all his story to the dewdrops glistening,
But naught they heard, for they are always listening,
The dewdrops, for the sound of their own dropping.
And then the man whom Sorrow named his friend,
Sought once again the shore, and found a shell
And thought, *I will my heavy story tell*
Till my own words, re-echoing, shall send
Their sadness through a hollow, pearly heart;
And my own tale again for me shall sing,
And my own whispering words be comforting
And lo! my ancient burden may depart.
Then he sang softly nigh the pearly rim;
But the sad dweller by the sea-ways lone
Changed all he sang to inarticulate moan
Among her wildering whirls, forgetting him.

THE CLOAK, THE BOAT,
AND THE SHOES

"What do you make so fair and bright?"

"I make the cloak of Sorrow:
O, lovely to see in all men's sight
Shall be the cloak of Sorrow,
In all men's sight."

"What do you build with sails for flight?"

"I build a boat for Sorrow,
O, swift on the seas all day and night
Saileth the rover Sorrow,
All day and night."

"What do you weave with wool so white?"

"I weave the shoes of Sorrow,
Soundless shall be the footfall light
In all men's ears of Sorrow,
Sudden and light."

ANASHUYA AND VIJAYA

A little Indian temple in the Golden Age.
Around it a garden; around that the forest.
ANASHUYA, *the young priestess, kneeling*
within the temple.

ANASHUYA. Send peace on all the lands and
    flickering corn.—
O, may tranquillity walk by his elbow
When wandering in the forest, if he love
No other.—Hear, and may the indolent flocks
Be plentiful.—And if he love another,
May panthers end him.—Hear, and load our king
With wisdom hour by hour.—May we two stand,
When we are dead, beyond the setting suns,
A little from the other shades apart,
With mingling hair, and play upon one lute.
    VIJAYA [*entering and throwing a lily at her*].
Hail! hail, my Anashuya.

                    No: be still.
I, priestess of this temple, offer up
Prayers for the land.
    VIJAYA.   I will wait here, Amrita.
    ANASHUYA. By mighty Brahma's ever rustling robe,
Who is Amrita? Sorrow of all sorrows!
Another fills your mind.
    VIJAYA.   My mother's name.
    ANASHUYA [*sings, coming out of the temple*].
A sad, sad thought went by me slowly:
Sigh, O you little stars! O, sigh and shake your blue
    apparel!
The sad, sad thought has gone from me now wholly:

Sing, O you little stars! O sing, and raise your
    rapturous carol
To mighty Brahma, he who made you many as the
    sands,
And laid you on the gates of evening with his quiet
    hands.
                    [*Sits down on the steps of the temple.*]
Vijaya, I have brought my evening rice;
The sun has laid his chin on the gray wood,
Weary, with all his poppies gathered round him.

 VIJAYA. The hour when Kama, full of sleepy
    laughter,
Rises, and showers abroad his fragrant arrows,
Piercing the twilight with their murmuring barbs.

 ANASHUYA, See how the sacred old flamingoes come,
Painting with shadow all the marble steps:
Aged and wise, they seek their wonted perches
Within the temple, devious walking, made
To wander by their melancholy minds.
Yon tall one eyes my supper; swiftly chase him
Far, far away. I named him after you.
He is a famous fisher; hour by hour
He ruffles with his bill the minnowed streams.
Ah! there he snaps my rice. I told you so.
Now cuff him off. He's off! A kiss for you,
Because you saved my rice. Have you no thanks?

 VIJAYA. [*sings*]. *Sing you of her, O first few stars,*
Whom Brahma, touching with his finger, praises, for
    you hold
the ran of wandering quiet; ere you be too calm and
    old,
Sing, turning in your cars,
Sing, till you raise your hands and sigh, and from your
    car heads peer,

—21—

With all your whirling hair, and drop tear upon azure
   tear.
  AANSHUYA. What know the pilots of the stars of
    tears?
  VIJAYA. Their faces are all worn, and in their
    eyes
Flashes the fire of sadness, for they see
The icicles that famish all the north,
Where men lie frozen in the glimmering snow;
And in the flaming forests cower the lion
And lioness, with all their whimpering cubs;
And, ever pacing on the verge of things,
The phantom, Beauty, in a mist of tears;
While we alone have round us woven woods,
And feel the softness of each other's hand,
Amrita, while——
  ANASHUYA [*going away from him*]. Ah me, you love
    another,
                        [*Bursting into tears.*]
And may some dreadful ill befall her quick!
  VIJAYA. I loved another; now I love no other.
Among the mouldering of ancient woods
You live, and on the village border she,
With her old father the blind wood-cutter;
I saw her standing in her door but now.
  ANASHUYA. Vijaya, swear to love her never more.
  VIJAYA. Ay, ay.
  ANASHUYA. Swear by the parents of the gods,
Dread oath, who dwell on sacred Himalay,
On the far Golden Peak; enormous shapes,
Who still were old when the great sea was young;
On their vast faces mystery and dreams;
Their hair along the mountains rolled and filled
From year to year by the unnumbered nests
Of aweless birds, and round their stirless feet

The joyous flocks of deer and antelope,
Who never hear the unforgiving hound.
Swear!

    VIJAYA. By the parents of the gods, I swear.

    ANASHUYA [*sings*]. *I have forgiven, O new star!*

Maybe you have not heard of us, you have come forth
    so newly,
You hunter of the fields afar!
Ah, you will know my loved one by his hunter's
    arrows truly,
Shoot on him shafts of quietness, that he may ever
    keep
An inner laughter, and may kiss his hands to me in
    sleep.

Farewell, Vijaya. Nay, no word, no word;
I, priestess of this temple, offer up
Prayers for the land.   [VIJAYA *goes.*]
                      O Brahma, guard in sleep
The merry lambs and the complacent kine,
The flies below the leaves, and the young mice
In the tree roots, and all the sacred flocks
Of red flamingo; and my love, Vijaya;
And may no restless fay with fidget finger
Trouble his sleeping: give him dreams of me.

THE INDIAN UPON GOD

I passed along the water's edge below the humid
    trees,
My spirit rocked in evening light, the rushes round my
    knees,
My spirit rocked in sleep and sighs; and saw the
    moorfowl pace
All dripping on a grassy slope, and saw them cease to
    chase
Each other round in circles, and heard the eldest
    speak:
*Who holds the world between His bill and made us
    strong or weak*
Is an undying moorfowl, and He lives beyond the sky.
*The rains are from His dripping wing, the moonbeams
    from his eye.*
I passed a little further on and heard a lotus talk:
*Who made the world and ruleth it, He hangeth on a
    stalk,*
For I am in His image made, and all this tinkling tide
Is but a sliding drop of rain between His petals wide.
A little way within the gloom a roebuck raised his eyes
Brimful of starlight, and he said: *The Stamper of the
    Skies,*
He is a gentle roebuck; for how else, I pray, could he
*Conceive a thing so sad and soft, a gentle thing like
    me?*
I passed a little further on and heard a peacock say:
*Who made the grass and made the worms and made
    my feathers gay,*
*He is a monstrous peacock, and He waveth all the
    night*
His languid tail above us, lit with myriad spots of light.

THE INDIAN TO HIS LOVE

The island dreams under the dawn
And great boughs drop tranquillity;
The peahens dance on a smooth lawn,
A parrot sways upon a tree,
Raging at his own image in the enamelled
     sea.

Here we will moor our lonely ship
And wander ever with woven hands,
Murmuring softly lip to lip,
Along the grass, along the sands,
Murmuring how far away are the unquiet
     lands:

How we alone of mortals are
Hid under quiet boughs apart,
While our love grows an Indian star,
A meteor of the burning heart,
One with the tide that gleams, the wings that
     gleam and dart,

The heavy boughs, the burnished dove
That moans and sighs a hundred days:
How when we die our shades will rove,
When eve has hushed the feathered ways,
Dropping a vapoury footsole on the tide's
     drowsy blaze.

THE FALLING OF THE LEAVES

Autumn is over the long leaves that love us,
And over the mice in the barley sheaves;
Yellow the leaves of the rowan above us,
And yellow the wet wild-strawberry leaves.

The hour of the waning of love has beset us,
And weary and worn are our sad souls now;
Let us part, ere the season of passion forget us,
With a kiss and a tear on thy drooping brow.

EPHEMERA

"Your eyes that once were never weary of mine
Are bowed in sorrow under their trembling lids,
Because our love is waning."
                              And then she:
"Although our love is waning, let us stand
By the lone border of the lake once more,
Together in that hour of gentleness
When the poor tired child, Passion, falls asleep:
How far away the stars seem, and how far
Is our first kiss, and ah, how old my heart!"
Pensive they paced along the faded leaves,
While slowly he whose hand held hers replied:
"Passion has often worn our wandering hearts."

The woods were round them, and the yellow leaves
Fell like faint meteors in the gloom, and once
A rabbit old and lame limped down the path;
Autumn was over him: and now they stood
On the lone border of the lake once more:
Turning, he saw that she had thrust dead leaves
Gathered in silence, dewy as her eyes,
In bosom and hair.
                    "Ah, do not mourn," he said,
"That we are tired, for other loves await us:
Hate on and love through unrepining hours;
Before us lies eternity; our souls
Are love, and a continual farewell."

THE MADNESS OF KING GOLL

I sat on cushioned otter skin:
My word was law from Ith to Emen,
And shook at Invar Amargin
The hearts of the world-troubling seamen,
And drove tumult and war away
From girl and boy and man and beast;
The fields grew fatter day by day,
The wild fowl of the air increased;
And every ancient Ollave said,
While he bent down his fading head,
"He drives away the Northern cold."
They will not hush, the leaves a-flutter round
me, the beech leaves old.

I sat and mused and drank sweet wine;
A herdsman came from inland valleys,
Crying, the pirates drove his swine
To fill their dark-beaked hollow galleys.
I called my battle-breaking men,
And my loud brazen battle-cars
From rolling vale and rivery glen;
And under the blinking of the stars
Fell on the pirates by the deep,
And hurled them in the gulph of sleep:
These hands won many a torque of gold.
They will not hush, the leaves a-flutter round
me, the beech leaves old.

But slowly, as I shouting slew
And trampled in the bubbling mire,
In my most secret spirit grew
A whirling and a wandering fire:

I stood: keen stars above me shone,
Around me shone keen eyes of men:
I laughed aloud and hurried on
By rocky shore and rushy fen;
I laughed because birds fluttered by,
And starlight gleamed, and clouds flew high,
And rushes waved and waters rolled.
They will not hush, the leaves a-flutter round
me, the beech leaves old.

And now I wander in the woods
When summer gluts the golden bees,
Or in autumnal solitudes
Arise the leopard-coloured trees;
Or when along the wintry strands
The cormorants shiver on their rocks;
I wander on, and wave my hands,
And sing, and shake my heavy locks.
The gray wolf knows me; by one ear
I lead along the woodland deer;
The hares run by me growing bold.
They will not hush, the leaves a-flutter round
me, the beech leaves old.

I came upon a little town,
That slumbered in the harvest moon,
And passed a-tiptoe up and down,
Murmuring, to a fitful tune,
How I have followed, night and day,
A tramping of tremendous feet,
And saw where this old tympan lay,
Deserted on a doorway seat,
And bore it to the woods with me;

Of some unhuman misery
Our married voices wildly trolled.
They will not hush, the leaves a-flutter round
me, the beech leaves old.

I sang how, when day's toil is done,
Orchil shakes out her long dark hair
That hides away the dying sun
And sheds faint odours through the air:
When my hand passed from wire to wire
It quenched, with sound like falling dew,
The whirling and the wandering fire;
But lift a mournful ulalu,
For the kind wires are torn and still,
And I must wander wood and hill
Through summer's heat and winter's cold.
They will not hush, the leaves a-flutter round
me, the beech leaves old.

THE STOLEN CHILD

Where dips the rocky highland
Of Sleuth Wood in the lake,
There lies a leafy island
Where flapping herons wake
The drowsy water rats;
There we've hid our faery vats.
Full of berries,
And of reddest stolen cherries.
Come away, O human child!
To the waters and the wild
With a faery, hand in hand,
For the world's more full of weeping
than you can understand.

Where the wave of moonlight glosses
The dim gray sands with light,
Far off by furthest Rosses
We foot it all the night,
Weaving olden dances,
Mingling hands and mingling glances
Till the moon has taken flight;
To and fro we leap
And chase the frothy bubbles,
While the world is full of troubles
And is anxious in its sleep.
Come away, O human child!
To the waters and the wild
With a faery, hand in hand,
For the world's more full of weeping
than you can understand.

Where the wandering water gushes
From the hills above Glen-Car,
In pools among the rushes
That scarce could bathe a star,
We seek for slumbering trout,
And whispering in their ears
Give them unquiet dreams;
Leaning softly out
From ferns that drop their tears
Over the young streams,
Come away, O human child!
To the waters and the wild
With a faery, hand in hand,
For the world's more full of weeping
    than you can understand.

Away with us he's going,
The solemn-eyed:
He'll hear no more the lowing
Of the calves on the warm hillside;
Or the kettle on the hob
Sing peace into his breast,
Or see the brown mice bob
Round and round the oatmeal-chest.
For he comes, the human child,
To the waters and the wild
With a faery, hand in hand,
From a world more full of weeping than
    he can understand.

TO AN ISLE
IN THE WATER

Shy one, shy one,
Shy one of my heart,
She moves in the firelight
Pensively apart.

She carries in the dishes,
And lays them in a row.
To an isle in the water
With her would I go.

She carries in the candles,
And lights the curtained room,
Shy in the doorway
And shy in the gloom;

And shy as a rabbit,
Helpful and shy.
To an isle in the water
With her would I fly.

DOWN BY THE SALLEY GARDENS

Down by the salley gardens my love and I
    did meet;
She passed the salley gardens with little snow-
    white feet.
She bid me take love easy, as the leaves grow
    on the tree;
But I, being young and foolish, with her
    would not agree.

In a field by the river my love and I did
    stand,
And on my leaning shoulder she laid her
    snow-white hand.
She bid me take life easy, as the grass grows
    on the weirs;
But I was young and foolish, and now am full
    of tears.

THE MEDITATION OF THE OLD FISHERMAN

You waves, though you dance by my feet
    like children at play,
Though you glow and you glance, though you
    purr and you dart;
In the Junes that were warmer than these are,
    the waves were more gay,
When I was a boy with never a crack in my
    heart.

The herring are not in the tides as they were
    of old;
My sorrow! for many a creak gave the creel
    in the cart
That carried the take to Sligo town to be sold,
When I was a boy with never a crack in my
    heart.

And ah, you proud maiden, you are not so
    fair when his oar
Is heard on the water, as they were, the proud
    and apart,
Who paced in the eve by the nets on the
    pebbly shore,
When I was a boy with never a crack in my
    heart.

THE BALLAD OF FATHER O'HART

Good Father John O'Hart
In penal days rode out
To a shoneen who had free lands
And his own snipe and trout.

In trust took he John's lands;
Sleiveens were all his race;
And he gave them as dowers to his daughters,
And they married beyond their place.

But Father John went up,
And Father John went down;
And he wore small holes in his shoes,
And he wore large holes in his gown.

All loved him, only the shoneen,
Whom the devils have by the hair,
From the wives, and the cats, and the children,
To the birds in the white of the air.

The birds, for he opened their cages
As he went up and down;
And he said with a smile, "Have peace now;"
And he went his way with a frown.

But if when any one died
Came keeners hoarser than rooks,
He bade them give over their keening;
For he was a man of books.

And these were the works of John,
When weeping score by score,
People came into Coloony;
For he'd died at ninety-four.

There was no human keening;
The birds from Knocknarea
And the world round Knocknashee
Came keening in that day.

The young birds and old birds
Came flying, heavy and sad;
Keening in from Tiraragh,
Keening from Ballinafad;

Keening from Inishmurray,
Nor stayed for bite or sup;
This way were all reproved
Who dig old customs up.

THE BALLAD OF MOLL MAGEE

Come round me, little childer;
There, don't fling stones at me
Because I mutter as I go;
But pity Moll Magee.

My man was a poor fisher
With shore lines in the say;
My work was saltin' herrings
The whole of the long day.

And sometimes from the saltin' shed,
I scarce could drag my feet
Under the blessed moonlight,
Along the pebbly street.

I'd always been but weakly,
And my baby was just born;
A neighbour minded her by day,
I minded her till morn.

I lay upon my baby;
Ye little childer dear,
I looked on my cold baby
When the morn grew frosty and clear.

A weary woman sleeps so hard!
My man grew red and pale,
And gave me money, and bade me go
To my own place Kinsale.

He drove me out and shut the door,
And gave his curse to me;

I went away in silence,
No neighbour could I see.

The windows and the doors were shut,
One star shone faint and green;
The little straws were turnin' round
Across the bare boreen.

I went away in silence:
Beyond old Martin's byre
I saw a kindly neighbour
Blowin' her mornin' fire

She drew from me my story—
My money's all used up,
And still, with pityin', scornin' eye,
She gives me bite and sup.

She says my man will surely come,
And fetch me home agin;
But always, as I'm movin' round,
Without doors or within,

Pilin' the wood or pilin' the turf,
Or goin' to the well,
I'm thinkin' of my baby
And keenin' to mysel'.

And sometimes I am sure she knows
When, openin' wide His door,
God lights the stars, His candles,
And looks upon the poor.

So now, ye little childer,
Ye won't fling stones at me;
But gather with your shinin' looks
And pity Moll Magee.

THE BALLAD OF THE FOXHUNTER

"Now lay me in a cushioned chair
And carry me, you four,
With cushions here and cushions there,
To see the world once more.
And some one from the stables bring
My Dermot dear and brown,
And lead him gently in a ring,
And gently up and down.

"Now leave the chair upon the grass;
Bring hound and huntsman here,
And I on this strange road will pass,
Filled full of ancient cheer."
His eyelids droop, his head falls low,
His old eyes cloud with dreams;
The sun upon all things that grow
Pours round in sleepy streams.

Brown Dermot treads upon the lawn,
And to the armchair goes,
And now the old man's dreams are gone,
He smooths the long brown nose.

And now moves many a pleasant tongue
Upon his wasted hands,
For leading aged hounds and young
The huntsman near him stands.

"My huntsman, Rody, blow the horn,
And make the hills reply."
The huntsman loosens on the morn
A gay and wandering cry.

A fire is in the old man's eyes,
His fingers move and sway,
And when the wandering music dies
They hear him feebly say,

"My huntsman, Rody, blow the horn,
And make the hills reply,"
"I cannot blow upon my horn,
I can but weep and sigh."

The servants round his cushioned place
Are with new sorrow wrung;
And hounds are gazing on his face,
Both aged hounds and young.

One blind hound only lies apart
On the sun-smitten grass;
He holds deep commune with his heart:
The moments pass and pass;

The blind hound with a mournful din
Lifts slow his wintry head;
The servants bear the body in;
The hounds wail for the dead.

Early Poems

— II —

THE ROSE

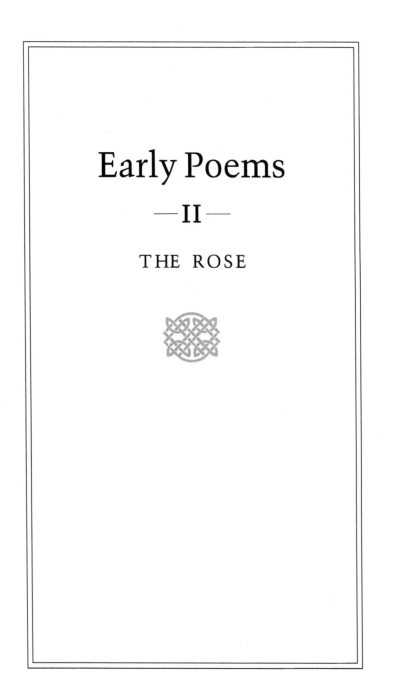

TO THE ROSE UPON
THE ROOD OF TIME

Red Rose, proud Rose, sad Rose of all my days!
Come near me, while I sing the ancient ways:
Cuchulain battling with the bitter tide;
The Druid, gray, wood-nurtured, quiet-eyed,
Who cast round Fergus dreams, and ruin
    untold;
And thine own sadness, whereof stars, grown old
In dancing silver sandalled on the sea,
Sing in their high and lonely melody.
Come near, that no more blinded by man's fate,
I find under the boughs of love and hate,
In all poor foolish things that live a day,
Eternal beauty wandering on her way.

Come near, come near, come near—Ah, leave
    me still
A little space for the rose-breath to fill!
Lest I no more hear common things that crave;
The weak worm hiding down in its small cave,
The field mouse running by me in the grass,
And heavy mortal hopes that toil and pass;
But seek alone to hear the strange things said
By God to the bright hearts of those long dead,
And learn to chaunt a tongue men do not know.
Come near; I would, before my time to go,
Sing of old Eire and the ancient ways:
Red Rose, proud Rose, sad Rose of all my days.

FERGUS AND THE DRUID

FERGUS. The whole day have I followed
   in the rocks,
And you have changed and flowed from shape
   to shape.
First as a raven on whose ancient wings
Scarcely a feather lingered, then you seemed
A weasel moving on from stone to stone,
And now at last you wear a human shape,
A thin gray man half lost in gathering night.

   DRUID. What would you, king of the proud
     Red Branch kings?
   FERGUS. This would I say, most wise of
     living souls:
Young subtle Conchubar sat close by me
When I gave judgment, and his words were
   wise,
And what to me was burden without end,
To him seemed easy, so I laid the crown
Upon his head to cast away my care.
   DRUID. What would you, king of the proud
     Red Branch kings?
   FERGUS. I feast amid my people on the
     hill,
And pace the woods, and drive my chariot
   wheels
In the white border of the murmuring
   sea;
And still I feel the crown upon my head.
   DRUID. What would you, king of the proud
     Red Branch kings?

FERGUS. I'd put away the foolish might
    of a king,
But learn the dreaming wisdom that is yours.
    DRUID. Look on my thin grey hair and hol-
    low cheeks,
And on these hands that may not lift the
    sword
This body trembling like a wind-blown reed.
No maiden loves me, no man seeks my help,
Because I be not of the things I dream.
    FERGUS. A wild and foolish labourer is a
    king,
To do and do and do, and never dream.
    DRUID. Take, if you must, this little bag of
    dreams;
Unloose the cord, and they will wrap you
    round.
    FERGUS. I see my life go dripping like a
    stream
From change to change; I have been many
    things,
A green drop in the surge, a gleam of light
Upon a sword, a fir-tree on a hill,
An old slave grinding at a heavy quern,
A king sitting upon a chair of gold,
And all these things were wonderful and great;
But now I have grown nothing, being all,
And the whole world weighs down upon my
    heart:
Ah! Druid, Druid, how great webs of sorrow
Lay hidden in the small slate-coloured thing!

THE DEATH OF CUCHULAIN

A man came slowly from the setting sun,
To Forgail's daughter, Emer, in her dun,
And found her dyeing cloth with subtle care,
And said, casting aside his draggled hair:
"I am Aleel, the swineherd, whom you bid
Go dwell upon the sea cliffs, vapour hid;
But now my years of watching are no more."

Then Emer cast the web upon the floor,
And stretching out her arms, red with the dye,
Parted her lips with a loud sudden cry.

Looking on her, Aleel, the swineherd, said:
"Not any god alive, nor mortal dead,
Has slain so mighty armies, so great kings,
Nor won the gold that now Cuchulain brings."

"Why do you tremble thus from feet to crown?"

Aleel, the swineherd, wept and cast him down
Upon the web-heaped floor, and thus his word:
"With him is one sweet throated like a bird,
And lovelier than the moon upon the sea;
He made for her an army cease to be."

"Who bade you tell these things?" and then she cried
To those about, "Beat him with thongs of hide
And drive him from the door." And thus it was:
And where her son, Finmole, on the smooth grass
Was driving cattle, came she with swift feet,
And called out to him, "Son, it is not meet
That you stay idling here with flocks and herds."

"I have long waited, mother, for those words;
But wherefore now?"

                "There is a man to die;
You have the heaviest arm under the sky."

"My father dwells among the sea-worn bands,
And breaks the ridge of battle with his hands."

"Nay, you are taller than Cuchulain, son."
"He is the mightiest man in ship or dun."

"Nay, he is old and sad with many wars,
And weary of the crash of battle cars."

"I only ask what way my journey lies,
For God, who made you bitter, made you wise."

"The Red Branch kings a tireless banquet keep.
Where the sun falls into the Western deep.
Go there, and dwell on the green forest rim
But tell alone your name and house to him
Whose blade compels, and bid them send you one
Who has a like vow from their triple dun."

Between the lavish shelter of a wood
And the gray tide, the Red Branch multitude
Feasted, and with them old Cuchulain dwelt,
And his young dear one close beside him knelt,
  nd gazed upon the wisdom of his eyes,
    ·e mournful than the depth of starry skies,
     ondered on the wonder of his days;
      around the harp-string told his praise,
       hubar, the Red Branch king of kings,
        ·n fingers touched the brazen strings.
        lain spake, "A young man strays

Driving the deer along the woody ways.
I often hear him singing to and fro
I often hear the sweet sound of his bow,
Seek out what man he is."

                    One went and came.
"He bade me let all know he gives his name
At the sword point, and bade me bring him one
Who had a like vow from our triple dun."

"I only of the Red Branch hosted now,"
Cuchulain cried, "have made and keep that vow."

After short fighting in the leafy shade,
He spake to the young man, "Is there no maid
Who loves you, no white arms to wrap you round,
Or do you long for the dim sleepy ground,
That you come here to meet this ancient sword?"

"The dooms of men are in God's hidden hoard."

"Your head a while seemed like a woman's head
That I loved once."

                    Again the fighting sped,
But now the war rage in Cuchulain woke,
And through the other's shield his long blade broke,
And pierced him.

                "Speak before your breath is done."

"I am Finmole, mighty Cuchulain's son."

"I put you from your pain. I can no more."

While day its burden on to evening bore,
With head bowed on his knees Cuchulain stayed;
Then Conchubar sent that sweet-throated maid,
And she, to win him, his gray hair caressed;
In vain her arms, in vain her soft white breast.
Then Conchubar, the subtlest of all men,
Ranking his Druids round him ten by ten,
Spake thus, "Cuchulain will dwell there and brood,
For three days more in dreadful quietude,
And then arise, and raving slay us all.
Go, cast on him delusions magical,
That he might fight the waves of the loud sea."
And ten by ten under a quicken tree,
The Druids chaunted, swaying in their hands
Tall wands of alder and white quicken wands.

In three days' time, Cuchulain with a moan
Stood up, and came to the long sands alone:
For four days warred he with the bitter tide;
And the waves flowed above him, and he died.

THE ROSE OF THE WORLD

Who dreamed that beauty passes like a
    dream?
For these red lips, with all their mournful
    pride,
Mournful that no new wonder may betide,
Troy passed away in one high funeral gleam,
And Usna's children died.

We and the labouring world are passing by:
Amid men's souls, that waver and give place,
Like the pale waters in their wintry race,
Under the passing stars, foam of the sky,
Lives on this lonely face.

Bow down, archangels, in your dim abode:
Before you were, or any hearts to beat,
Weary and kind one lingered by His seat;
He made the world to be a grassy road
Before her wandering feet.

THE ROSE OF PEACE

If Michael, leader of God's host
When Heaven and Hell are met,
Looked down on you from Heaven's door-post
He would his deeds forget.

Brooding no more upon God's wars
In his Divine homestead,
He would go weave out of the stars
A chaplet for your head.

And all folk seeing him bow down,
And white stars tell your praise,
Would come at last to God's great town,
Led on by gentle ways;

And God would bid His warfare cease.
Saying all things were well;
And softly make a rosy peace,
A peace of Heaven with Hell.

THE ROSE OF BATTLE

Rose of all Roses, Rose of all the World!
The tall thought-woven sails, that flap un-
    furled
Above the tide of hours, trouble the air,
And God's bell buoyed to be the water's care;
While hushed from fear, or loud with hope, a
    band
With blown, spray-dabbled hair gather at
    hand.
Turn if you may from battles never done,
I call, as they go by me one by one,
Danger no refuge holds, and war no peace,
For him who hears love sing and never cease,
Beside her clean-swept hearth, her quiet shade:
But gather all for whom no love hath made
A woven silence, or but came to cast
A song into the air, and singing past
To smile on the pale dawn; and gather you
Who have sought more than is in rain or dew
Or in the sun and moon, or on the earth,
Or sighs amid the wandering, starry mirth,
Or comes in laughter from the sea's sad lips;
And wage God's battles in the long gray ships.
The sad, the lonely, the insatiable,
To these Old Night shall all her mystery tell;
God's bell has claimed them by the little cry
Of their sad hearts, that may not live nor die.

Rose of all Roses, Rose of all the World!
You, too, have come where the dim tides are
    hurled
Upon the wharves of sorrow, and heard ring

The bell that calls us on; the sweet far thing.
Beauty grown sad with its eternity
Made you of us, and of the dim gray sea.
Our long ships loose thought-woven sails and
    wait,
For God has bid them share an equal fate;
And when at last defeated in His wars,
They have gone down under the same white
    stars,
We shall no longer hear the little cry
Of our sad hearts, that may not live nor die.

A FAERY SONG

*Sung by the people of faery over Diarmuid and
Grania, who lay in their bridal sleep under
a Cromlech.*

We who are old, old and gay,
O so old!
Thousands of years, thousands of years
If all were told:

Give to these children, new from the world,
Silence and love;
And the long dew-dropping hours of the night,
And the stars above:

Give to these children, new from the world,
Rest far from men.
Is anything better, anything better?
Tell us it then:

Us who are old, old and gay:
O so old!
Thousands of years, thousands of years,
If all were told.

THE LAKE ISLE OF INNISFREE

I will arise and go now, and go to Innisfree,
And a small cabin build there, of clay and
    wattles made;
Nine bean rows will I have there, a hive for the
    honey bee,
And live alone in the bee-loud glade.

And I shall have some peace there, for peace
    comes dropping slow,
Dropping from the veils of the morning to
    where the cricket sings;
There midnight's all a glimmer, and noon a
    purple glow,
And evening full of the linnet's wings.

I will arise and go now, for always night and
    day
I hear lake water lapping with low sounds by
    the shore;
While I stand on the roadway, or on the pave-
    ments gray,
I hear it in the deep heart's core.

A CRADLE SONG

The angels are stooping
Above your bed;
They weary of trooping
With the whimpering dead.

God's laughing in heaven
To see you so good;
The Shining Seven
Are gay with His mood.

I kiss you and kiss you,
My pigeon, my own;
Ah, how I shall miss you
When you have grown.

THE PITY OF LOVE

A pity beyond all telling
Is hid in the heart of love:
The folk who are buying and selling;
The clouds on their journey above;
The cold wet winds ever blowing;
And the shadowy hazel grove
Where mouse-gray waters are flowing
Threaten the head that I love.

THE SORROW OF LOVE

The quarrel of the sparrows in the eaves,
The full round moon and the star-laden sky,
And the loud song of the ever-singing leaves,
Had hid away earth's old and weary cry.

And then you came with those red mournful lips,
And with you came the whole of the world's tears,
And all the trouble of her labouring ships,
And all the trouble of her myriad years.

And now the sparrows warring in the eaves,
The curd-pale moon, the white stars in the sky,
And the loud chaunting of the unquiet leaves,
Are shaken with earth's old and weary cry.

WHEN YOU ARE OLD

When you are old and gray and full of sleep,
And nodding by the fire, take down this book,
And slowly read, and dream of the soft look
Your eyes had once, and of their shadows deep;

How many loved your moments of glad grace,
And loved your beauty with love false or true;
But one man loved the pilgrim soul in you,
And loved the sorrows of your changing face.

And bending down beside the glowing bars
Murmur, a little sadly, how love fled
And paced upon the mountains overhead
And hid his face amid a crowd of stars.

THE WHITE BIRDS

I would that we were, my beloved, white birds
 on the foam of the sea!
We tire of the flame of the meteor, before it
 can fade and flee;
And the flame of the blue star of twilight,
 hung low on the rim of the sky,
Has awaked in our hearts, my beloved, a sad-
 ness that may not die.

A weariness comes from those dreamers, dew
 dabbled, the lily and rose;
Ah, dream not of them, my beloved, the flame
 of the meteor that goes,
Or the flame of the blue star that lingers hung
 low in the fall of the dew:
For I would we were changed to white birds
 on the wandering foam: I and you!

I am haunted by numberless islands, and
 many a Danaan shore,
Where Time would surely forget us, and Sor-
 row come near us no more;
Soon far from the rose and the lily, and fret
 of the flames would we be,
Were we only white birds, my beloved, buoyed
 out on the foam of the sea!

A DREAM OF DEATH

I dreamed that one had died in a strange place
Near no accustomed hand;
And they had nailed the boards above her face
The peasants of that land,
And, wondering, planted by her solitude
A cypress and a yew:
I came, and wrote upon a cross of wood,
Man had no more to do:
She was more beautiful than thy first love,
This lady by the trees:
And gazed upon the mournful stars above,
And heard the mournful breeze.

A DREAM OF
A BLESSED SPIRIT

All the heavy days are over;
Leave the body's coloured pride
Underneath the grass and clover,
With the feet laid side by side.

One with her are mirth and duty;
Bear the gold embroidered dress,
For she needs not her sad beauty,
To the scented oaken press.

Hers the kiss of Mother Mary,
The long hair is on her face;
Still she goes with footsteps wary,
Full of earth's old timid grace.

With white feet of angels seven
Her white feet go glimmering;
And above the deep of heaven,
Flame on flame and wing on wing.

THE MAN WHO DREAMED
OF FAERYLAND

He stood among a crowd at Drumahair;
His heart hung all upon a silken dress,
And he had known at last some tenderness,
Before earth made of him her sleepy care;
But when a man poured fish into a pile,
It seemed they raised their little silver heads,
And sang how day a Druid twilight sheds
Upon a dim, green, well-beloved isle,
Where people love beside star-laden seas;
How Time may never mar their faery vows
Under the woven roofs of quicken boughs:
The singing shook him out of his new ease.

He wandered by the sands of Lisadill;
His mind ran all on money cares and fears,
And he had known at last some prudent years
Before they heaped his grave under the hill;
But while he passed before a plashy place,
A lug-worm with its gray and muddy mouth
Sang how somewhere to north or west or south
There dwelt a gay, exulting, gentle race;
And how beneath those three times blessed skies
A Danaan fruitage makes a shower of moons,
And as it falls awakens leafy tunes:
And at that singing he was no more wise.

He mused beside the well of Scanavin,
He mused upon his mockers: without fail
His sudden vengeance were a country tale,
Now that deep earth has drunk his body in;
But one small knot-grass growing by the pool
Told where, ah, little, all-unneeded voice!

Old Silence bids a lonely folk rejoice,
And chaplet their calm brows with leafage cool;
And how, when fades the sea-strewn rose of day,
A gentle feeling wraps them like a fleece,
And all their trouble dies into its peace:
The tale drove his fine angry mood away.

He slept under the hill of Lugnagall;
And might have known at last unhaunted sleep
Under that cold and vapour-turbaned steep,
Now that old earth had taken man and all:
Were not the worms that spired about his bones
A-telling with their low and reedy cry,
Of how God leans His hands out of the sky,
To bless that isle with honey in His tones;
That none may feel the power of squall and wave,
And no one any leaf-crowned dancer miss
Until He burn up Nature with a kiss:
The man has found no comfort in the grave.

THE DEDICATION TO
A BOOK OF STORIES SELECTED FROM
THE IRISH NOVELISTS

There was a green branch hung with many a bell
When her own people ruled in wave-worn Eire;
And from its murmuring greenness, calm of faery,
A Druid kindness, on all hearers fell.

It charmed away the merchant from his guile,
And turned the farmer's memory from his cattle,
And hushed in sleep the roaring ranks of battle,
For all who heard it dreamed a little while.

Ah, Exiles wandering over many seas,
Spinning at all times Eire's good tomorrow!
Ah, worldwide Nation, always growing Sorrow!
I also bear a bell branch full of ease.

I tore it from green boughs winds tossed and hurled,
Green boughs of tossing always, weary, weary!
I tore it from the green boughs of old Eire,
The willow of the many-sorrowed world.

Ah, Exiles, wandering over many lands!
My bell branch murmurs: the gay bells bring laughter,
Leaping to shake a cobweb from the rafter;
The sad bells bow the forehead on the hands.

A honeyed ringing: under the new skies
They bring you memories of old village faces;
Cabins gone now, old well-sides, old dear places;
And men who loved the cause that never dies.

THE LAMENTATION OF
THE OLD PENSIONER

I had a chair at every hearth,
When no one turned to see,
With "Look at that old fellow there,
And who may he be?"
And therefore do I wander now,
And the fret lies on me.

The road-side trees keep murmuring
Ah, wherefore murmur ye,
As in the old days long gone by,
Green oak and poplar tree?
The well-known faces are all gone
And the fret lies on me.

THE BALLAD OF
FATHER GILLIGAN

The old priest Peter Gilligan
Was weary night and day;
For half his flock were in their beds,
Or under green sods lay.

Once, while he nodded on a chair,
At the moth-hour of eve,
Another poor man sent for him,
And he began to grieve.

"I have no rest, nor joy, nor peace,
For people die and die";
And after cried he, "God forgive!
My body spake, not I!"

He knelt, and leaning on the chair
He prayed and fell asleep;
And the moth-hour went from the fields,
And stars began to peep.

They slowly into millions grew,
And leaves shook in the wind;
And God covered the world with shade,
And whispered to mankind.

Upon the time of sparrow chirp
When the moths came once more,
The old priest Peter Gilligan
Stood upright on the floor.

"Mavrone, mavrone! the man has died,
While I slept on the chair";
He roused his horse out of its sleep,
And rode with little care.

He rode now as he never rode,
By rocky lane and fen;
The sick man's wife opened the door:
'Father! you come again!'

"And is the poor man dead?" he cried.
"He died an hour ago,"
The old priest Peter Gilligan
In grief swayed to and fro.

"When you were gone, he turned and died
As merry as a bird."
The old priest Peter Gilligan
He knelt him at that word.

"He who hath made the night of stars
For souls, who tire and bleed,
Sent one of His great angels down
To help me in my need.

"He who is wrapped in purple robes,
With planets in His care,
Had pity on the least of things
Asleep upon a chair."

THE TWO TREES

Beloved, gaze in thine own heart,
The holy tree is growing there;
From joy the holy branches start,
And all the trembling flowers they bear.
The changing colours of its fruit
Have dowered the stars with merry light;
The surety of its hidden root
Has planted quiet in the night;
The shaking of its leafy head
Has given the waves their melody,
And made my lips and music wed,
Murmuring a wizard song for thee.
There, through bewildered branches, go
Winged Loves borne on in gentle strife,
Tossing and tossing to and fro
The flaming circle of our life.
When looking on their shaken hair,
And dreaming how they dance and dart,
Thine eyes grow full of tender care:
Beloved, gaze in thine own heart.

Gaze no more in the bitter glass
The demons, with their subtle guile,
Lift up before us when they pass,
Or only gaze a little while;
For there a fatal image grows,
With broken boughs, and blackened leaves,
And roots half hidden under snows
Driven by a storm that ever grieves.
For all things turn to barrenness

In the dim glass the demons hold,
The glass of outer weariness,
Made when God slept in times of old.
There, through the broken branches, go
The ravens of unresting thought;
Peering and flying to and fro,
To see men's souls bartered and bought.
When they are heard upon the wind,
And when they shake their wings; alas!
Thy tender eyes grow all unkind:
Gaze no more in the bitter glass.

TO IRELAND IN THE COMING TIMES

Know, that I would accounted be
True brother of that company,
Who sang to sweeten Ireland's wrong,
Ballad and story, rann and song;
Nor be I any less of them,
Because the red-rose-bordered hem
Of her, whose history began
Before God made the angelic clan,
Trails all about the written page;
For in the world's first blossoming age
The light fall of her flying feet
Made Ireland's heart begin to beat;
And still the starry candles flare
To help her light foot here and there;
And still the thoughts of Ireland brood
Upon her holy quietude.

Nor may I less be counted one
With Davis, Mangan, Ferguson,
Because to him, who ponders well,
My rhymes more than their rhyming tell
Of the dim wisdoms old and deep,
That God gives unto man in sleep.
For the elemental beings go
About my table to and fro.
In flood and fire and clay and wind,
They huddle from man's pondering mind;
Yet he who treads in austere ways
May surely meet their ancient gaze.
Man ever journeys on with them
After the red-rose-bordered hem.
Ah, faeries, dancing under the moon,
A Druid land, a Druid tune!

While still I may, I write for you
The love I lived, the dream I knew.
From our birthday, until we die,
Is but the winking of an eye;
And we, our singing and our love,
The mariners of night above,
And all the wizard things that go
About my table to and fro,
Are passing on to where may be,
In truth's consuming ecstasy,
No place for love and dream at all;
For God goes by with white foot-fall.
I cast my heart into my rhymes,
That you, in the dim coming times,
May know how my heart went with them
After the red-rose-bordered hem.

The Wind
Among the Reeds

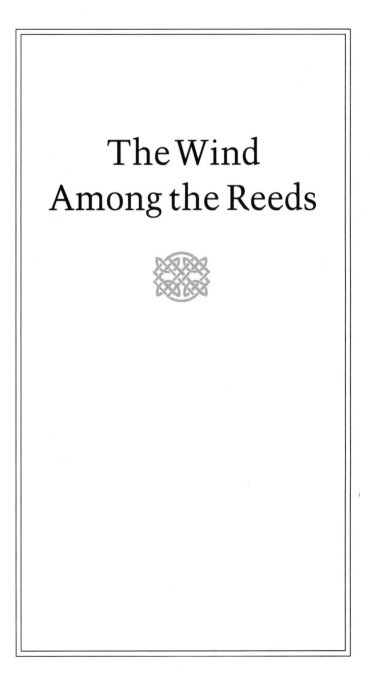

THE HOSTING OF THE SIDHE

The host is riding from Knocknarea
And over the grave of Clooth-na-bare;
Caolte tossing his burning hair
And Niamh calling *Away, come away:*
Empty your heart of its mortal dream.
The winds awaken, the leaves whirl round,
Our cheeks are pale, our hair is unbound,
Our breasts are heaving, our eyes are a-gleam,
Our arms are waving, our lips are apart;
And if any gaze on our rushing band,
We come between him and the deed of his hand,
We come between him and the hope of his heart.
The host is rushing 'twixt night and day,
And where is there hope or deed as fair?
Caolte tossing his burning hair,
And Niamh calling *Away, come away.*

THE EVERLASTING VOICES

O sweet everlasting voices be still;
Go to the guards of the heavenly fold
And bid them wander obeying your will
Flame under flame, till Time be no more;
Have you not heard that our hearts are old,
That you call in birds, in wind on the hill,
In shaken boughs, in tide on the shore?
O sweet everlasting Voices be still.

THE MOODS

Time drops in decay,
Like a candle burnt out,
And the mountains and woods
Have their day, have their day;
What one in the rout
Of the fire-born moods,
Has fallen away?

THE LOVER TELLS OF
THE ROSE IN HIS HEART

All things uncomely and broken, all things
    worn out and old,
The cry of a child by the roadway, the creak
    of a lumbering cart,
The heavy steps of the ploughman, splashing
    the wintry mould,
Are wronging your image that blossoms a
    rose in the deeps of my heart.

The wrong of unshapely things is a wrong too
    great to be told;
I hunger to build them anew and sit on a
    green knoll apart,
With the earth and the sky and the water,
    remade, like a casket of gold
For my dreams of your image that blossoms
    a rose in the deeps of my heart.

THE HOST OF THE AIR

O'Driscoll drove with a song,
The wild duck and the drake,
From the tall and the tufted reeds
Of the drear Hart Lake.

And he saw how the reeds grew dark
At the coming of night tide,
And dreamed of the long dim hair
Of Bridget his bride.

He heard while he sang and dreamed
A piper piping away,
And never was piping so sad,
And never was piping so gay.

And he saw young men and young girls
Who danced on a level place
And Bridget his bride among them,
With a sad and a gay face.

The dancers crowded about him,
And many a sweet thing said,
And a young man brought him red wine
And a young girl white bread.

But Bridget drew him by the sleeve,
Away from the merry bands,
To old men playing at cards
With a twinkling of ancient hands.

The bread and the wine had a doom,
For these were the host of the air;

He sat and played in a dream
Of her long dim hair.

He played with the merry old men
And thought not of evil chance,
Until one bore Bridget his bride
Away from the merry dance.

He bore her away in his arms,
The handsomest young man there,
And his neck and his breast and his arms
Were drowned in her long dim hair.

O'Driscoll scattered the cards
And out of his dream awoke:
Old men and young men and young girls
Were gone like a drifting smoke;

But he heard high up in the air
A piper piping away,
And never was piping so sad,
And never was piping so gay.

THE FISHERMAN

Although you hide in the ebb and flow
Of the pale tide when the moon has set,
The people of coming days will know
About the casting out of my net,
And how you have leaped times out of mind
Over the little silver cords,
And think that you were hard and unkind,
And blame you with many bitter words.

A CRADLE SONG

The Danaan children laugh, in cradles of
    wrought gold,
And clap their hands together, and half close
    their eyes,
For they will ride the North when the ger-
    eagle flies,
With heavy whitening wings, and a heart
    fallen cold:
I kiss my wailing child and press it to my
    breast,
And hear the narrow graves calling my child
    and me.

Desolate winds that cry over the wandering
    sea;
Desolate winds that hover in the flaming
    West;
Desolate winds that beat the doors of
    Heaven, and beat
The doors of Hell and blow there many a
    whimpering ghost;
O heart the winds have shaken; the unap-
    peasable host
Is comelier than candles at Mother Mary's
    feet.

INTO THE TWILIGHT

Out-worn heart, in a time out-worn,
Come clear of the nets of wrong and right;
Laugh heart again in the gray twilight,
Sigh, heart, again in the dew of the morn.

Your mother Eire is always young,
Dew ever shining and twilight gray;
Though hope fall from you and love decay,
Burning in fires of a slanderous tongue.

Come, heart, where hill is heaped upon hill:
For there the mystical brotherhood
Of sun and moon and hollow and wood
And river and stream work out their will;

And God stands winding His lonely horn,
And time and the world are ever in flight;
And love is less kind than the gray twilight,
And hope is less dear than the dew of the morn.

THE SONG OF
WANDERING AENGUS

I went out to the hazel wood,
Because a fire was in my head,
And cut and peeled a hazel wand,
And hooked a berry to a thread;
And when white moths were on the wing,
And moth-like stars were flickering out,
I dropped the berry in a stream
And caught a little silver trout.

When I had laid it on the floor
I went to blow the fire a-flame,
But something rustled on the floor,
And some one called me by my name:
It had become a glimmering girl
With apple blossom in her hair
Who called me by my name and ran
And faded through the brightening air.

Though I am old with wandering
Through hollow lands and hilly lands,
I will find out where she has gone,
And kiss her lips and take her hands;
And walk among long dappled grass,
And pluck till time and times are done,
The silver apples of the moon,
The golden apples of the sun.

THE SONG OF
THE OLD MOTHER

I rise in the dawn, and I kneel and blow
Till the seed of the fire flicker and glow;
And then I must scrub and bake and sweep
Till stars are beginning to blink and peep;
And the young lie long and dream in their bed
Of the matching of ribbons for bosom and head,
And their day goes over in idleness,
And they sigh if the wind but lift a tress:
While I must work because I am old,
And the seed of the fire gets feeble and cold.

THE FIDDLER OF DOONEY

When I play on my fiddle in Dooney,
Folk dance like a wave of the sea;
My cousin is priest in Kilvarnet,
My brother in Moharabuiee.

I passed my brother and cousin:
They read in their books of prayer;
I read in my book of songs
I bought at the Sligo fair.

When we come at the end of time,
To Peter sitting in state,
He will smile on the three old spirits,
But call me first through the gate;

For the good are always the merry,
Save by an evil chance,
And the merry love the fiddle
And the merry love to dance:

And when the folk there spy me,
They will all come up to me,
With "Here is the fiddler of Dooney!"
And dance like a wave of the sea.

THE HEART OF THE WOMAN

O what to me the little room
That was brimmed up with prayer and rest;
He bade me out into the gloom,
And my breast lies upon his breast.

O what to me my mother's care,
The house where I was safe and warm;
The shadowy blossom of my hair
Will hide us from the bitter storm.

O hiding hair and dewy eyes,
I am no more with life and death,
My heart upon his warm heart lies,
My breath is mixed into his breath.

THE LOVER MOURNS FOR
THE LOSS OF LOVE

Pale brows, still hands and dim hair,
I had a beautiful friend
And dreamed that the old despair
Would end in love in the end:
She looked in my heart one day
And saw your image was there;
She has gone weeping away.

HE MOURNS FOR THE CHANGE THAT HAS COME UPON HIM AND HIS BELOVED AND LONGS FOR THE END OF THE WORLD

Do you not hear me calling, white deer with no horns!
I have been changed to a hound with one red ear;
I have been in the Path of Stones and the Wood of
    Thorns,
For somebody hid hatred and hope and desire and
    fear
Under my feet that they follow you night and day.
A man with a hazel wand came without sound;
He changed me suddenly; I was looking another way;
And now my calling is but the calling of a hound;
And Time and Birth and Change are hurrying by.
I would that the Boar without bristles had come from
    the West
And had rooted the sun and moon and stars out of the
    sky
And lay in the darkness, grunting, and turning to his
    rest.

HE BIDS HIS BELOVED BE AT PEACE

I hear the Shadowy Horses, their long manes a-shake,
Their hoofs heavy with tumult, their eyes glimmering
    white;
The North unfolds above them clinging, creeping
    night,
The East her hidden joy before the morning break,
The West weeps in pale dew and sighs passing away,
The South is pouring down roses of crimson fire:
O vanity of Sleep, Hope, Dream, endless Desire,
The Horses of Disaster plunge in the heavy clay:
Beloved, let your eyes half close, and your heart beat
Over my heart, and your hair fall over my breast,
Drowning love's lonely hour in deep twilight of rest,
And hiding their tossing manes and their tumultuous
    feet.

HE REPROVES THE CURLEW

O, curlew, cry no more in the air,
Or only to the waters in the West;
Because your crying brings to my mind
Passion-dimmed eyes and long heavy hair
That was shaken out over my breast:
There is enough evil in the crying of wind.

HE REMEMBERS FORGOTTEN BEAUTY

When my arms wrap you round I press
My heart upon the loveliness
That has long faded from the world;
The jewelled crowns that kings have hurled
In shadowy pools, when armies fled;
The love-tales wrought with silken thread
By dreaming ladies upon cloth
That has made fat the murderous moth;
The roses that of old time were
Woven by ladies in their hair,
The dew-cold lilies ladies bore
Through many a sacred corridor
Where such gray clouds of incense rose
That only the gods' eyes did not close:
For that pale breast and lingering hand
Come from a more dream-heavy land,
A more dream-heavy hour than this;
And when you sigh from kiss to kiss
I hear white Beauty sighing, too,
For hours when all must fade like dew
But flame on flame, deep under deep,
Throne over throne, where in half sleep
Their swords upon their iron knees
Brood her high lonely mysteries.

A POET TO HIS BELOVED

I bring you with reverent hands
The books of my numberless dreams;
White woman that passion has worn
As the tide wears the dove-gray sands,
And with heart more old than the horn
That is brimmed from the pale fire of time:
White woman with numberless dreams
I bring you my passionate rhyme.

HE GIVES HIS BELOVED
CERTAIN RHYMES

Fasten your hair with a golden pin,
And bind up every wandering tress;
I bade my heart build these poor rhymes:
It worked at them, day out, day in,
Building a sorrowful loveliness
Out of the battles of old times.

You need but lift a pearl-pale hand,
And bind up your long hair and sigh;
And all men's hearts must burn and beat;
And candle-like foam on the dim sand,
And stars climbing the dew-dropping sky,
Live but to light your passing feet.

TO MY HEART,
BIDDING IT HAVE NO FEAR

Be you still, be you still, trembling heart;
Remember the wisdom out of the old days:
Him who trembles before the flame and the flood,
And the winds that blow through the starry ways,
Let the starry winds and the flame and the flood
Cover over and hide, for he has no part
With the proud, majestical multitude.

THE CAP AND BELLS

The jester walked in the garden:
The garden had fallen still;
He bade his soul rise upward
And stand on her windowsill.

It rose in a straight blue garment,
When owls began to call:
It had grown wise-tongued by thinking
Of a quiet and light footfall;

But the young queen would not listen;
She rose in her pale nightgown;
She drew in the heavy casement
And pushed the latches down.

He bade his heart go to her,
When the owls called out no more;
In a red and quivering garment
It sang to her through the door.

It had grown sweet-tongued by dreaming,
Of a flutter of flower-like hair;
But she took up her fan from the table
And waved it off on the air.

"I have cap and bells," he pondered,
"I will send them to her and die;"
And when the morning whitened
He left them where she went by.

She laid them upon her bosom,
Under a cloud of her hair,
And her red lips sang them a love song:
Till stars grew out of the air.

She opened her door and her window,
And the heart and the soul came through,
To her right hand came the red one,
To her left hand came the blue.

They set up a noise like crickets,
A chattering wise and sweet,
And her hair was a folded flower
And the quiet of love in her feet.

THE VALLEY OF THE BLACK PIG

The dews drop slowly and dreams gather:
    unknown spears
Suddenly hurtle before my dream-awakened
    eyes,
And then the clash of fallen horsemen and
    the cries
Of unknown perishing armies beat about my
    ears.
We who still labour by the cromlec on the
    shore,
The grey cairn on the hill, when day sinks
    drowned in dew,
Being weary of the world's empires, bow down
    to you
Master of the still stars and of the flaming
    door.

THE LOVER ASKS FORGIVENESS
BECAUSE OF HIS MANY MOODS

If this importunate heart trouble your peace
With words lighter than air,
Or hopes that in mere hoping flicker and cease;
Crumple the rose in your hair;
And cover your lips with odorous twilight and say,
"O Hearts of wind-blown flame!
O Winds, elder than changing of night and day,
That murmuring and longing came,
From marble cities loud with tabors of old
In dove-gray faery lands;
From battle banners fold upon purple fold,
Queens wrought with glimmering hands;
That saw young Niamh hover with love-lorn face
Above the wandering tide;
And lingered in the hidden desolate place,
Where the last Phœnix died
And wrapped the flames above his holy head;
And still murmur and long:
O Piteous Hearts, changing till change be dead
In a tumultuous song:"
And cover the pale blossoms of your breast
With your dim heavy hair,
And trouble with a sigh for all things longing for rest
The odorous twilight there.

HE TELLS OF A VALLEY
FULL OF LOVERS

I dreamed that I stood in a valley, and amid
sighs,
For happy lovers passed two by two where I
stood;
And I dreamed my lost love came stealthily
out of the wood
With her cloud-pale eyelids falling on dream-
dimmed eyes:
I cried in my dream "*O women, bid the young
men lay*
*Their heads on your knees, and drown their
eyes with your hair,*
*Or remembering hers they will find no other
face fair*
*Till all the valleys of the world have been with-
ered away.*"

HE TELLS OF THE PERFECT BEAUTY

O cloud-pale eyelids, dream-dimmed eyes
The poets labouring all their days
To build a perfect beauty in rhyme
Are overthrown by a woman's gaze
And by the unlabouring brood of the skies:
And therefore my heart will bow, when dew
Is dropping sleep, until God burn time,
Before the unlabouring stars and you.

HE HEARS THE CRY
OF THE SEDGE

I wander by the edge
Of this desolate lake
Where wind cries in the sedge
Until the axle break
That keeps the stars in their round,
And hands hurl in the deep
The banners of East and West,
And the girdle of light is unbound,
Your breast will not lie by the breast
Of your beloved in sleep.

HE THINKS OF THOSE WHO HAVE
SPOKEN EVIL OF HIS BELOVED

Half close your eyelids, loosen your hair,
And dream about the great and their pride;
They have spoken against you everywhere,
But weigh this song with the great and their pride;
I made it out of a mouthful of air,
Their children's children shall say they have lied.

THE BLESSED

Cumhal called out, bending his head,
Till Dathi came and stood,
With a blink in his eyes at the cave mouth,
Between the wind and the wood.

And Cumhal said, bending his knees,
"I have come by the windy way
To gather the half of your blessedness
And learn to pray when you pray.

"I can bring you salmon out of the streams
And heron out of the skies."
But Dathi folded his hands and smiled
With the secrets of God in his eyes.

And Cumhal saw like a drifting smoke
All manner of blessed souls,
Women and children, young men with books,
And old men with croziers and stoles.

"Praise God and God's mother," Dathi said,
"For God and God's mother have sent
The blessedest souls that walk in the world
To fill your heart with content."

"And which is the blessedest," Cumhal said,
"Where all are comely and good?
Is it these that with golden thuribles
Are singing about the wood?"

"My eyes are blinking," Dathi said,
"With the secrets of God half blind,
But I can see where the wind goes
And follow the way of the wind;

"And blessedness goes where the wind goes,
And when it is gone we are dead;
I see the blessedest soul in the world
And he nods a drunken head.

"O blessedness comes in the night and the day
And whither the wise heart knows;
And one has seen in the redness of wine
The Incorruptible Rose,

"That drowsily drops faint leaves on him
And the sweetness of desire,
While time and the world are ebbing away
In twilights of dew and of fire."

THE SECRET ROSE

Far off, most secret, and inviolate Rose,
Enfold me in my hour of hours; where those
Who sought thee in the Holy Sepulchre,
Or in the wine vat, dwell beyond the stir
And tumult of defeated dreams; and deep
Among pale eyelids, heavy with the sleep
Men have named beauty. Thy great leaves enfold
The ancient beards, the helms of ruby and gold
Of the crowned Magi; and the king whose eyes
Saw the Pierced Hands and Rood of elder rise
In druid vapour and make the torches dim;
Till vain frenzy awoke and he died; and him
Who met Fand walking among flaming dew
By a gray shore where the wind never blew,
And lost the world and Emer for a kiss;
And him who drove the gods out of their liss,
And till a hundred morns had flowered red,
Feasted and wept the barrows of his dead;
And the proud dreaming king who flung the crown
And sorrow away, and calling bard and clown
Dwelt among wine-stained wanderers in deep woods;
And him who sold tillage, and house, and goods,
And sought through lands and islands numberless years,
Until he found with laughter and with tears,
A woman, of so shining loveliness,
That men threshed corn at midnight by a tress,
A little stolen tress. I, too, await
The hour of thy great wind of love and hate.
When shall the stars be blown about the sky,
Like the sparks blown out of a smithy, and die?
Surely thine hour has come, thy great wind blows,
Far off, most secret, and inviolate Rose?

THE LOVER MOURNS BECAUSE
OF HIS WANDERINGS

O where is our Mother of Peace
Nodding her purple hood?
For the winds that awakened the stars
Are blowing through my blood.
I would that the death-pale deer
Had come through the mountain side,
And trampled the mountain away,
And drunk up the murmuring tide;
For the winds that awakened the stars
Are blowing through my blood,
And our Mother of Peace has forgot me
Under her purple hood.

THE TRAVAIL OF PASSION

When the flaming lute-thronged angelic door is wide;
When an immortal passion breathes in mortal clay;
Our hearts endure the scourge, the plaited thorns, the way
Crowded with bitter faces, the wounds in palm and side,
The hyssop-heavy sponge, the flowers by Kidron stream;
We will bend down and loosen our hair over you,
That it may drop faint perfume, and be heavy with dew,
Lilies of death-pale hope, roses of passionate dream.

THE LOVER PLEADS WITH
HIS FRIEND FOR OLD FRIENDS

Though you are in your shining days,
Voices among the crowd
And new friends busy with your praise,
Be not unkind or proud,
But think about old friends the most:
Time's bitter flood will rise,
Your beauty perish and be lost
For all eyes but these eyes.

A LOVER SPEAKS TO THE HEARERS
OF HIS SONGS IN COMING DAYS

O, women, kneeling by your altar rails long hence,
When songs I wove for my beloved hide the prayer,
And smoke from this dead heart drifts through the violet
    air
And covers away the smoke of myrrh and frankincense;
Bend down and pray for the great sin I wove in song,
Till Mary of the wounded heart cry a sweet cry,
And call to my beloved and me: "No longer fly
Amid the hovering, piteous, penitential throng."

THE POET PLEADS WITH THE
ELEMENTAL POWERS

The Powers whose name and shape no living creature
    knows
Have pulled the Immortal Rose;
And though the Seven Lights bowed in their dance
    and wept,
The Polar Dragon slept,
His heavy rings uncoiled from glimmering deep to
    deep:
When will he wake from sleep?

Great Powers of falling wave and wind and windy fire,
With your harmonious choir
Encircle her I love and sing her into peace,
That my old care may cease;
Unfold your flaming wings and cover out of sight
The nets of day and night.

Dim Powers of drowsy thought, let her no longer be
Like the pale cup of the sea,
When winds have gathered and sun and moon burned
    dim
Above its cloudy rim;
But let a gentle silence wrought with music flow
Whither her footsteps go.

HE WISHES HIS BELOVED
WERE DEAD

Were you but lying cold and dead,
And lights were paling out of the West,
You would come hither, and bend your head,
And I would lay my head on your breast;
And you would murmur tender words,
Forgiving me, because you were dead:
Nor would you rise and hasten away,
Though you have the will of the wild birds,
But know your hair was bound and wound
About the stars and moon and sun:
O would beloved that you lay
Under the dock-leaves in the ground,
While lights were paling one by one.

HE WISHES FOR THE
CLOTHS OF HEAVEN

Had I the heavens' embroidered cloths,
Enwrought with golden and silver light,
The blue and the dim and the dark cloths
Of night and light and the half light,
I would spread the cloths under your feet:
But I, being poor, have only my dreams;
I have spread my dreams under your feet;
Tread softly because you tread on my dreams.

HE THINKS OF HIS PAST GREATNESS
WHEN A PART OF THE
CONSTELLATIONS OF HEAVEN

I have drunk ale from the Country of the Young
And weep because I know all things now:
I have been a hazel tree and they hung
The Pilot Star and the Crooked Plough
Among my leaves in times out of mind:
I became a rush that horses tread:
I became a man, a hater of the wind,
Knowing one, out of all things, alone, that his head
Would not lie on the breast or his lips on the hair
Of the woman that he loves, until he dies;
Although the rushes and the fowl of the air
Cry of his love with their pitiful cries.

In the
Seven Woods

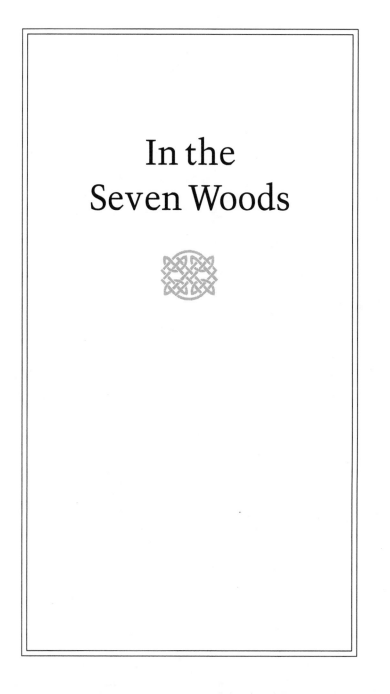

IN THE SEVEN WOODS

I have heard the pigeons of the Seven Woods
Make their faint thunder, and the garden bees
Hum in the lime tree flowers; and put away
The unavailing outcries and the old bitterness
That empty the heart. I have forgot awhile
Tara uprooted, and new commonness
Upon the throne and crying about the streets
And hanging its paper flowers from post to post,
Because it is alone of all things happy.
I am contented for I know that Quiet
Wanders laughing and eating her wild heart
Among pigeons and bees, while that Great Archer,
Who but awaits His hour to shoot, still hangs
A cloudy quiver over Parc-na-Lee.

August, 1902

THE ARROW

I thought of your beauty, and this arrow,
Made out of a wild thought, is in my marrow.
There's no man may look upon her, no man;
As when newly grown to be a woman,

Blossom pale, she pulled down the pale blossom
At the moth hour and hid it in her bosom.
This beauty's kinder yet for a reason
I could weep that the old is out of season.

THE FOLLY OF BEING COMFORTED

One that is ever kind said yesterday:
"Your well beloved's hair has threads of gray,
And little shadows come about her eyes;
Time can but make it easier to be wise,
Though now it's hard, till trouble is at an end;
And so be patient, be wise and patient, friend."
But heart, there is no comfort, not a grain;
Time can but make her beauty over again,
Because of that great nobleness of hers;
The fire that stirs about her, when she stirs
Burns but more clearly. O she had not these ways,
When all the wild summer was in her gaze.
O heart! O heart! if she'd but turn her head,
You'd know the folly of being comforted.

OLD MEMORY

I thought to fly to her when the end of day
Awakens an old memory, and say,
"Your strength, that is so lofty and fierce and kind,
It might call up a new age, calling to mind
The queens that were imagined long ago,
Is but half yours: he kneaded in the dough
Through the long years of youth, and who would have
    thought
It all, and more than it all, would come to naught,
And that dear words meant nothing?" But enough,
For when we have blamed the wind we can blame
    love:
Or, if there needs be more, be nothing said
That would be harsh for children that have strayed.

NEVER GIVE ALL THE HEART

Never give all the heart, for love
Will hardly seem worth thinking of
To passionate women, if it seem
Certain, and they never dream
That it fades out from kiss to kiss;
For everything that's lovely is
But a brief dreamy kind delight.
O never give the heart outright
For they, for all smooth lips can say,
Have given their hearts up to the play.
And who could play it well enough
If deaf and dumb and blind with love?
He that made this knows all the cost
For he gave all his heart and lost.

THE WITHERING OF THE BOUGHS

I cried when the moon was murmuring to the
    birds,
"Let peewit call and curlew cry where they
    will,
I long for your merry and tender and pitiful
    words,
For the roads are unending, and there is no
    place to my mind."
The honey-pale moon lay low on the sleepy
    hill,
And I fell asleep upon lonely Echtge of
    streams.
No boughs have withered because of the
    wintry wind;
The boughs have withered because I have
    told them my dreams.

I know of the leafy paths that the witches
    take,
Who come with their crowns of pearl and
    their spindles of wool,
And their secret smile, out of the depths
    of the lake;
I know where a dim moon drifts, where the
    Danaan kind
Wind and unwind their dances when the
    light grows cool
On the island lawns, their feet where the
    pale foam gleams.

No boughs have withered because of the
    wintry wind;
The boughs have withered because I have told
    them my dreams.

I know of the sleepy country, where swans fly
    round
Coupled with golden chains, and sing as they
    fly.
A king and a queen are wandering there, and
    the sound
Has made them so happy and hopeless, so
    deaf and so blind
With wisdom, they wander till all the years
    have gone by;
I know, and the curlew and peewit on Echtge
    of streams.

No boughs have withered because of the wintry
    wind;
The boughs have withered because I have
    told them my dreams.

ADAM'S CURSE

We sat together at one summer's end,
That beautiful mild woman, your close friend,
And you and I, and talked of poetry.

I said: "A line will take us hours maybe;
Yet if it does not seem a moment's thought,
Our stitching and unstitching has been
        naught.
Better go down upon your marrow bones
And scrub a kitchen pavement, or break
        stones
Like an old pauper, in all kinds of weather;
For to articulate sweet sounds together
Is to work harder than all these, and yet
Be thought an idler by the noisy set
Of bankers, schoolmasters, and clergymen
The martyrs call the world."

                            That woman then
Murmured with her young voice, for whose
        mild sake
There's many a one shall find out all heartache
In finding that it's young and mild and low:
"There is one thing that all we women know,
Although we never heard of it at school—
That we must labour to be beautiful."

I said: "It's certain there is no fine thing
Since Adam's fall but needs much labouring.
There have been lovers who thought love
        should be
So much compounded of high courtesy

That they would sigh and quote with learned
     looks
Precedents out of beautiful old books;
Yet now it seems an idle trade enough."

We sat grown quiet at the name of love;
We saw the last embers of daylight die,
And in the trembling blue-green of the sky
A moon, worn as if it had been a shell
Washed by time's waters as they rose and fell
About the stars and broke in days and years.

I had a thought for no one's but your ears;
That you were beautiful, and that I strove
To love you in the old highway of love;
That it had all seemed happy, and yet we'd
     grown
As weary hearted as that hollow moon.

RED HANRAHAN'S SONG
ABOUT IRELAND

The old brown thorn trees break in two high
  over Cummen Strand,
Under a bitter black wind that blows from
  the left hand;
Our courage breaks like an old tree in a black
  wind and dies,
But we have hidden in our hearts the flame
  out of the eyes
Of Cathleen, the daughter of Houlihan.

The wind has bundled up the clouds high over
  Knocknarea,
And thrown the thunder on the stones for all
  that Maeve can say.
Angers that are like noisy clouds have set our
  hearts abeat;
But we have all bent low and low and kissed
  the quiet feet
Of Cathleen, the daughter of Houlihan.

The yellow pool has overflowed high up on
  Clooth-na-Bare,
For the wet winds are blowing out of the
  clinging air;
Like heavy flooded waters our bodies and our
  blood
But purer than a tall candle before the Holy
  Rood
Is Cathleen, the daughter of Houlihan.

THE OLD MEN ADMIRING
THEMSELVES IN THE WATER

I heard the old, old men say,
"Everything alters,
And one by one we drop away."
They had hands like claws, and their knees
Were twisted like the old thorn trees
By the waters.
I heard the old, old men say,
"All that's beautiful drifts away
Like the waters."

UNDER THE MOON

I have no happiness in dreaming of Brycelinde,
Nor Avalon the grass-green hollow, nor Joyous Isle,
Where one found Lancelot crazed and hid him for a
    while;
Nor Ulad, when Naoise had thrown a sail upon the wind,
Nor lands that seem too dim to be burdens on the heart;
Land-under-Wave, where out of the moon's light and the
    sun's
Seven old sisters wind the threads of the longlived ones;
Land-of-the-Tower, where Aengus has thrown the gates
    apart,
And Wood-of-Wonders, where one kills an ox at dawn,
To find it when night falls laid on a golden bier:
Therein are many queens like Branwen and Guinivere;
And Niamh and Laban and Fand, who could change to
    an otter or fawn,
And the wood-woman, whose lover was changed to a
    blue-eyed hawk;
And whether I go in my dreams by woodland, or dun, or
    shore,
Or on the unpeopled waves with kings to pull at the oar,
I hear the harp-string praise them, or hear their mournful
    talk.
Because of a story I heard under the thin horn
Of the third moon, that hung between the night and the
    day,
To dream of women whose beauty was folded in dismay,
Even in an old story, is a burden not to be borne.

CHORUS FOR A PLAY

It is sung at the entrance of Deirdre into the House of the
Red Branch by certain wandering musicians. She
comes to the threshold at the end of the second verse,
and they, seeing her whispering to Naoise who is be-
side her, think that she is busy with her love, not
knowing that she is hesitating in fear.

    First Musician. Why is it, Queen Edain said,
If I do but climb the stair
To the tower overhead
When the winds are calling there,
Or the gannets calling out
In waste places of the sky,
There's so much to think about
That I cry, that I cry?
    Another Musician. But her goodman answered
      her:
Love would be a thing of naught
Had not all his limbs a stir
Born out of immoderate thought;
Were he anything by half;
Were his measures running dry.
Lovers if they may not laugh
Have to cry, have to cry.
    All the Musicians. But is Edain worth a song
Now the hunt begins anew?
Praise the beautiful and strong,
Praise the redness of the yew,
Praise the blossoming apple stem:
Yet our silence had been wise;
What is all our praise to them
That have one another's eyes?

THE PLAYERS ASK FOR
A BLESSING ON THE
PSALTERIES AND THEMSELVES

THREE VOICES TOGETHER. Hurry to bless the
     hands that play,
The mouths that speak, the notes and strings,
O masters of the glittering town!
O! lay the shrilly trumpet down,
Though drunken with the flags that sway
Over the ramparts and the towers,
And with the waving of your wings.
    FIRST VOICE. Maybe they linger by the way.
One gathers up his purple gown;
One leans and mutters by the wall—
He dreads the weight of mortal hours.
    SECOND VOICE. O no, O no! they hurry down
Like plovers that have heard the call.
    THIRD VOICE. O kinsmen of the Three in One,
O kinsmen bless the hands that play.
The notes they waken shall live on
When all this heavy history's done;
Our hands, our hands must ebb away.
    THREE VOICES TOGETHER. The proud and careless
     notes live on,
But bless our hands that ebb away.

THE HAPPY TOWNLAND

There's many a strong farmer
Whose heart would break in two,
If he could see the townland
That we are riding to;
Boughs have their fruit and blossom
At all times of the year;
Rivers are running over
With red beer and brown beer.
An old man plays the bagpipes
In a golden and silver wood;
Queens, their eyes blue like the ice,
Are dancing in the crowd.

The little fox he murmured,
"O what of the world's bane?"
The sun was laughing sweetly,
The moon plucked at my rein;
But the little red fox murmured,
"O do not pluck at his rein,
He is riding to the townland
That is the world's bane."

When their hearts are so high
That they would come to blows,
They unhook their heavy swords
From golden and silver boughs;
But all that are killed in battle
Awaken to life again:
It is lucky that their story
Is not known among men.
For O, the strong farmers
That would let the spade lie,

Their hearts would be like a cup
That somebody had drunk dry.

The little fox he murmured,
"O what of the world's bane?"
The sun was laughing sweetly,
The moon plucked at my rein;
But the little red fox murmured,
"O do not pluck at his rein,
He is riding to the townland
That is the world's bane."

Michael will unhook his trumpet
From a bough overhead,
And blow a little noise
When the supper has been spread.

Gabriel will come from the water
With a fish tail, and talk
Of wonders that have happened
On wet roads where men walk,
And lift up an old horn
Of hammered silver, and drink
Till he has fallen asleep
Upon the starry brink.

The little fox he murmured,
"O what of the world's bane?"
The sun was laughing sweetly,
The moon plucked at my rein;
But the little red fox murmured,
"O do not pluck at his rein,
He is riding to the townland
That is the world's bane."

The Old Age of
Queen Maeve

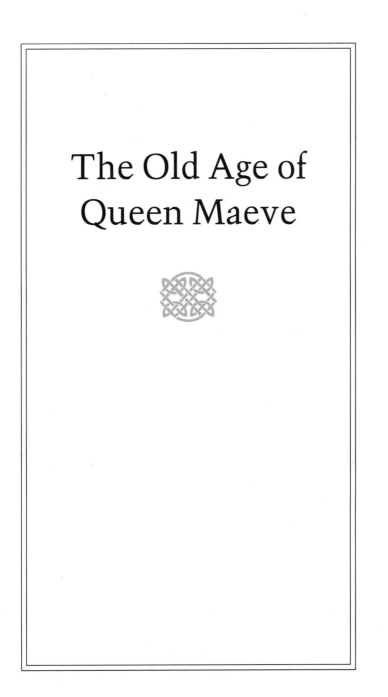

THE OLD AGE OF QUEEN MAEVE

Maeve the great queen was pacing to and fro,
Between the walls covered with beaten bronze,
In her high house at Cruachan; the long hearth,
Flickering with ash and hazel, but half showed
Where the tired horse-boys lay upon the rushes,
Or on the benches underneath the walls,
In comfortable sleep; all living slept
But that great queen, who more than half the night
Had paced from door to fire and fire to door.
Though now in her old age, in her young age
She had been beautiful in that old way
That's all but gone; for the proud heart is gone,
And the fool heart of the counting-house fears all
But soft beauty and indolent desire.
She could have called over the rim of the world
Whatever woman's lover had hit her fancy,
And yet had been great bodied and great limbed,
Fashioned to be the mother of strong children;
And she'd had lucky eyes and a high heart,
And wisdom that caught fire like the dried flax,
At need, and made her beautiful and fierce,
Sudden and laughing.
                              O unquiet heart,
Why do you praise another, praising her,
As if there were no tale but your own tale
Worth knitting to a measure of sweet sound?
Have I not bid you tell of that great queen
Who has been buried some two thousand years?

When night was at its deepest, a wild goose
Cried from the porter's lodge, and with long clamour
Shook the ale horns and shields upon their hooks;

But the horse-boys slept on, as though some power
Had filled the house with Druid heaviness;
And wondering who of the many changing Sidhe
Had come as in the old times to counsel her,
Maeve walked, yet with slow footfall, being old,
To that small chamber by the outer gate.
The porter slept, although he sat upright
With still and stony limbs and open eyes.
Maeve waited, and when that ear-piercing noise
Broke from his parted lips and broke again,
She laid a hand on either of his shoulders,
And shook him wide awake, and bid him say
Who of the wandering many-changing ones
Had troubled his sleep. But all he had to say
Was that, the air being heavy and the dogs
More still than they had been for a good month,
He had fallen asleep, and, though he had dreamed
    nothing,
He could remember when he had had fine dreams.
It was before the time of the great war
Over the White-Horned Bull, and the Brown Bull.

She turned away; he turned again to sleep
That no god troubled now, and, wondering
What matters were afoot among the Sidhe,
Maeve walked through that great hall, and with a sigh
Lifted the curtain of her sleeping room,
Remembering that she too had seemed divine
To many thousand eyes, and to her own
One that the generations had long waited
That work too difficult for mortal hands
Might be accomplished. Bunching the curtain up
She saw her husband Ailell sleeping there,
And thought of days when he'd had a straight body,
And of that famous Fergus, Nessa's husband,
Who had been the lover of her middle life.

Suddenly Ailell spoke out of his sleep,
And not with his own voice or a man's voice,
But with the burning, live, unshaken voice
Of those that it may be can never age.
He said, "High Queen of Cruachan and Magh Ai,
A king of the Great Plain would speak with you."
And with glad voice Maeve answered him, "What
    King
Of the far wandering shadows has come to me?
As in the old days when they would come and go
About my threshold to counsel and to help."
The parted lips replied, "I seek your help,
For I am Aengus, and I am crossed in love."

"How may a mortal whose life gutters out
Help them that wander with hand clasping hand,
Their haughty images that cannot wither
For all their beauty's like a hollow dream,
Mirrored in streams that neither hail nor rain
Nor the cold North has troubled?"
                      He replied
"I am from those rivers and I bid you call
The children of the Maines out of sleep,
And set them digging into Anbual's hill.
We shadows, while they uproot his earthy house,
Will overthrow his shadows and carry off
Caer, his blue-eyed daughter that I love.
I helped your fathers when they built these walls,
And I would have your help in my great need,
Queen of high Cruachan."
                 "I obey your will
With speedy feet and a most thankful heart:
For you have been, O Aengus of the birds,
Our giver of good counsel and good luck."
And with a groan, as if the mortal breath
Could but awaken sadly upon lips

That happier breath had moved, her husband turned
Face downward, tossing in a troubled sleep;
But Maeve, and not with a slow feeble foot,
Came to the threshold of the painted house,
Where her grandchildren slept, and cried aloud,
Until the pillared dark began to stir
With shouting and the clang of unhooked arms.

She told them of the many-changing ones;
And all that night, and all through the next day
To middle night, they dug into the hill.
At middle night great cats with silver claws,
Bodies of shadow and blind eyes like pearls,
Came up out of the hole, and red-eared hounds
With long white bodies came out of the air
Suddenly, and ran at them and harried them.

The Maines' children dropped their spades, and stood
With quaking joints and terror strucken faces,
Till Maeve called out: "These are but common men.
The Maines' children have not dropped their spades,
Because Earth, crazy for its broken power,
Casts up a show and the winds answer it
With holy shadows." Her high heart was glad,
And when the uproar ran along the grass
She followed with light footfall in the midst,
'Till it died out where an old thorn tree stood.

Friend of these many years, you too had stood
With equal courage in that whirling rout;
For you, although you've not her wandering heart,
Have all that greatness, and not hers alone.
For there is no high story about queens
In any ancient book but tells of you;
And when I've heard how they grew old and died,
Or fell into unhappiness, I've said:

"She will grow old and die, and she has wept!"
And when I'd write it out anew, the words,
Half crazy with the thought, She too has wept!
Outrun the measure.
                          I'd tell of that great queen
Who stood amid a silence by the thorn
Until two lovers came out of the air
With bodies made out of soft fire. The one,
About whose face birds wagged their fiery wings,
Said: "Aengus and his sweetheart give their thanks
To Maeve and to Maeve's household, owing all
In owing them the bride-bed that gives peace."
Then Maeve: "O Aengus, Master of all lovers,
A thousand years ago you held high talk
With the first kings of many pillared Cruachan.
O when will you grow weary?"
                          They had vanished;
But out of the dark air over her head there came
A murmur of soft words and meeting lips.

Baile and Aillinn

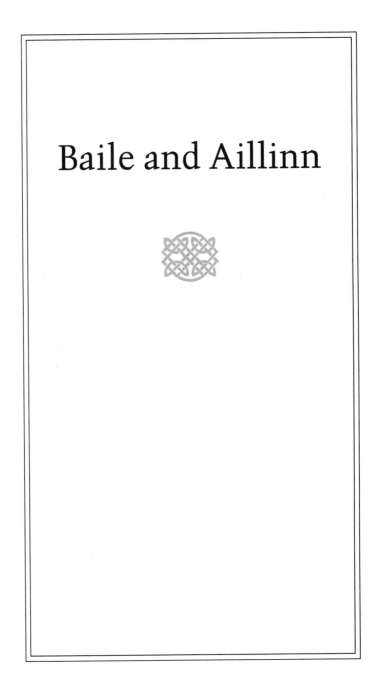

BAILE AND AILLINN

ARGUMENT. *Baile and Aillinn were lovers, but*
Aengus, the Master of Love, wishing them to
be happy in his own land among the dead,
told to each a story of the other's death, so
that their hearts were broken and they died.

I hardly hear the curlew cry,
Nor the gray rush when the wind is high,
Before my thoughts begin to run
On the heir of Ulad, Buan's son,
Baile, who had the honey mouth;
And that mild woman of the south,
Aillinn, who was King Lugaid's heir.
Their love was never drowned in care
Of this or that thing, nor grew cold
Because their bodies had grown old.
Being forbid to marry on earth,
They blossomed to immortal mirth.

About the time when Christ was born,
When the long wars for the White Horn
And the Brown Bull had not yet come,
Young Baile Honey-Mouth, whom some
Called rather Baile Little-Land,
Rode out of Emain with a band
Of harpers and young men; and they
Imagined, as they struck the way
To many pastured Muirthemne,
That all things fell out happily,
And there, for all that fools had said,
Baile and Aillinn would be wed.
They found an old man running there:

He had ragged long grass-coloured hair;
He had knees that stuck out of his hose;
He had puddle water in his shoes;
He had half a cloak to keep him dry,
Although he had a squirrel's eye.

O wandering birds and rushy beds,
You put such folly in our heads
With all this crying in the wind;
No common love is to our mind,
And our poor Kate or Nan is less
Than any whose unhappiness
Awoke the harp-strings long ago.
Yet they that know all things but know
That all life had to give us is
A child's laughter, a woman's kiss.
Who was it put so great a scorn
In the grey reeds that night and morn
Are trodden and broken by the herds,
And in the light bodies of birds
That north wind tumbles to and fro
And pinches among hail and snow?

That runner said: "I am from the south;
I run to Baile Honey-Mouth,
To tell him how the girl Aillinn
Rode from the country of her kin,
And old and young men rode with her:
For all that country had been astir
If anybody half as fair
Had chosen a husband anywhere
But where it could see her every day.
When they had ridden a little way
An old man caught the horse's head
With: 'You must home again, and wed
With somebody in your own land.'

A young man cried and kissed her hand,
'O lady, wed with one of us;'
And when no face grew piteous
For any gentle thing she spake,
She fell and died of the heart-break."

Because a lover's heart's worn out,
Being tumbled and blown about
By its own blind imagining,
And will believe that anything
That is bad enough to be true, is true,
Baile's heart was broken in two;
And he being laid upon green boughs,
Was carried to the goodly house
Where the Hound of Ulad sat before
The brazen pillars of his door,
His face bowed low to weep the end
Of the harper's daughter and her friend.
For although years had passed away
He always wept them on that day,
For on that day they had been betrayed;
And now that Honey-Mouth is laid
Under a cairn of sleepy stone
Before his eyes, he has tears for none,
Although he is carrying stone, but two
For whom the cairn's but heaped anew.

We hold because our memory is
So full of that thing and of this
That out of sight is out of mind.
But the grey rush under the wind
And the grey bird with crooked bill
Have such long memories, that they still
Remember Deirdre and her man;
And when we walk with Kate or Nan
About the windy water side,

Our heart can hear the voices chide.
How could we be so soon content,
Who know the way that Naoise went?
And they have news of Deirdre's eyes,
Who being lovely was so wise—
Ah! wise, my heart knows well how wise.

Now had that old gaunt crafty one,
Gathering his cloak about him, run
Where Aillinn rode with waiting maids,
Who amid leafy lights and shades
Dreamed of the hands that would unlace
Their bodies in some dim place
When they had come to the marriage bed;
And harpers, pondering with bowed head
A music that had thought enough
Of the ebb of all things to make love
Grow gentle without sorrowings;
And leather-coated men with slings
Who peered about on every side;
And amid leafy light he cried:
"He is well out of wind and wave;
They have heaped the stones above his grave
In Muirthemne, and over it
In changeless Ogham letters writ—

Baile, that was of Rury's seed.

But the gods long ago decreed
No waiting maid should ever spread
Baile and Aillinn's marriage bed,
For they should clip and clip again

Where wild bees hive on the Great Plain.
Therefore it is but little news
That put this hurry in my shoes."

And hurrying to the south, he came
To that high hill the herdsmen name
The Hill Seat of Leighin, because
Some god or king had made the laws
That held the land together there,
In old times among the clouds of the air.

That old man climbed; the day grew dim;
Two swans came flying up to him,
Linked by a gold chain each to each,
And with low murmuring laughing speech
Alighted on the windy grass.
They knew him: his changed body was
Tall, proud and ruddy, and light wings
Were hovering over the harp-strings
That Etain, Midhir's wife, had wove
In the hid place, being crazed by love.

What shall I call them? fish that swim,
Scale rubbing scale where light is dim
By a broad water-lily leaf;
Or mice in the one wheaten sheaf
Forgotten at the threshing place;
Or birds lost in the one clear space
Of morning light in a dim sky;
Or, it may be, the eyelids of one eye,
Or the door pillars of one house,
Or two sweet blossoming apple boughs
That have one shadow on the ground;
Or the two strings that made one sound
Where that wise harper's finger ran.
For this young girl and this young man

Have happiness without an end,
Because they have made so good a friend.

They know all wonders, for they pass
The towery gates of Gorias,
And Findrias and Falias,
And long-forgotten Murias,
Among the giant kings whose hoard
Cauldron and spear and stone and sword
Was robbed before Earth gave the wheat;
Wandering from broken street to street
They come where some huge watcher is,
And tremble with their love and kiss.

They know undying things, for they
Wander where earth withers away,
Though nothing troubles the great streams
But light from the pale stars, and gleams
From the holy orchards, where there is none
But fruit that is of precious stone,
Or apples of the sun and moon.

What were our praise to them: they eat
Quiet's wild heart, like daily meat,
Who when night thickens are afloat
On dappled skins in a glass boat,
Far out under a windless sky;
While over them birds of Aengus fly,
And over the tiller and the prow,
And waving white wings to and fro
Awaken wanderings of light air
To stir their coverlet and their hair.

And poets found, old writers say,
A yew tree where his body lay;
But a wild apple hid the grass

With its sweet blossom where hers was;
And being in good heart, because
A better time had come again
After the deaths of many men,
And that long fighting at the ford,
They wrote on tablets of thin board,
Made of the apple and the yew,
All the love stories that they knew.

Let rush and bird cry out their fill
Of the harper's daughter if they will,
Beloved, I am not afraid of her.
She is not wiser nor lovelier,
And you are more high of heart than she,
For all her wanderings over-sea;
But I'd have birds and rush forget
Those other two; for never yet
Has lover lived, but longed to wive
Like them that are no more alive.

The Green Helmet
and Other Poems

HIS DREAM

I swayed upon the gaudy stern
The butt end of a steering oar,
And everywhere that I could turn
Men ran upon the shore.

And though I would have hushed the crowd
There was no mother's son but said,
"What is the figure in a shroud
Upon a gaudy bed?"

And fishes bubbling to the brim
Cried out upon that thing beneath,
It had such dignity of limb,
By the sweet name of Death.

Though I'd my finger on my lip,
What could I but take up the song?
And fish and crowd and gaudy ship
Cried out the whole night long,

Crying amid the glittering sea,
Naming it with ecstatic breath,
Because it had such dignity
By the sweet name of Death.

A WOMAN HOMER SUNG

If any man drew near
When I was young,
I thought, "He holds her dear,"
And shook with hate and fear.
But oh, 't was bitter wrong
If he could pass her by
With an indifferent eye.

Whereon I wrote and wrought,
And now, being gray,
I dream that I have brought
To such a pitch my thought
That coming time can say,
"He shadowed in a glass
What thing her body was."

For she had fiery blood
When I was young,
And trod so sweetly proud
As 't were upon a cloud,
A woman Homer sung,
That life and letters seem
But an heroic dream.

THE CONSOLATION

I had this thought a while ago,
"My darling cannot understand
What I have done, or what would do
In this blind bitter land."

And I grew weary of the sun
Until my thoughts cleared up again,
Remembering that the best I have done
Was done to make it plain;

That every year I have cried, "At length
My darling understands it all,
Because I have come into my strength,
And words obey my call."

That had she done so who can say
What would have shaken from the sieve?
I might have thrown poor words away
And been content to live.

NO SECOND TROY

Why should I blame her that she filled my days
With misery, or that she would of late
Have taught to ignorant men most violent ways,
Or hurled the little streets upon the great,
Had they but courage equal to desire?
What could have made her peaceful with a mind
That nobleness made simple as a fire,
With beauty like a tightened bow, a kind
That is not natural in an age like this,
Being high and solitary and most stern?
Why, what could she have done being what she is?
Was there another Troy for her to burn?

RECONCILIATION

Some may have blamed you that you took away
The verses that could move them on the day
When, the ears being deafened, the sight of the eyes
    blind
With lightning you went from me, and I could find
Nothing to make a song about but kings,
Helmets, and swords, and half-forgotten things
That were like memories of you—but now
We'll out, for the world lives as long ago;
And while we're in our laughing, weeping fit,
Hurl helmets, crowns, and swords into the pit.
But, dear, cling close to me; since you were gone,
My barren thoughts have chilled me to the bone.

KING AND NO KING

"Would it were anything but merely voice!"
The No King cried who after that was King,
Because he had not heard of anything
That balanced with a word is more than noise;
Yet Old Romance being kind, let him prevail
Somewhere or somehow that I have forgot,
Though he'd but cannon—Whereas we that had
    thought
To have lit upon as clean and sweet a tale
Have been defeated by that pledge you gave
In momentary anger long ago;
And I that have not your faith, how shall I know
That in the blinding light beyond the grave
We'll find so good a thing as that we have lost?
The hourly kindness, the day's common speech,
The habitual content of each with each
When neither soul nor body has been crossed.

PEACE

Ah, that Time could touch a form
That could show what Homer's age
Bred to be a hero's wage.
"Were not all her life but storm,
Would not painters paint a form
Of such noble lines," I said.
"Such a delicate high head,
So much sterness and such charm,
Till they had changed us to like strength?"
Ah, but peace that comes at length,
Came when Time had touched her form.

AGAINST UNWORTHY PRAISE

O heart, be at peace, because
Nor knave nor dolt can break
What's not for their applause,
Being for a woman's sake.
Enough if the work has seemed,
So did she your strength renew,
A dream that a lion had dreamed
Till the wilderness cried aloud,
A secret between you two,
Between the proud and the proud.

What, still you would have their praise!
But here's a haughtier text,
The labyrinth of her days
That her own strangeness perplexed;
And how what her dreaming gave
Earned slander, ingratitude,
From self-same dolt and knave;
Aye, and worse wrong than these.
Yet she, singing upon her road,
Half lion, half child, is at peace.

THE FASCINATION OF
WHAT'S DIFFICULT

The fascination of what's difficult
Has dried the sap out of my veins, and rent
Spontaneous joy and natural content
Out of my heart. There's something ails our colt
That must, as if it had not holy blood,
Nor on an Olympus leaped from cloud to cloud,
Shiver under the lash, strain, sweat and jolt
As though it dragged road metal. My curse on plays
That have to be set up in fifty ways,
On the day's war with every knave and dolt,
Theatre business, management of men.
I swear before the dawn comes round again
I'll find the stable and pull out the bolt.

A DRINKING SONG

Wine comes in at the mouth
And love comes in at the eye;
That's all we shall know for truth
Before we grow old and die.
I lift the glass to my mouth,
I look at you, and I sigh.

THE COMING OF WISDOM
WITH TIME

Though leaves are many, the root is one;
Through all the lying days of my youth
I swayed my leaves and flowers in the sun;
Now I may wither into the truth.

ON HEARING THAT THE STUDENTS OF OUR NEW UNIVERSITY HAVE JOINED THE ANCIENT ORDER OF HIBERNIANS AND THE AGITATION AGAINST IMMORAL LITERATURE

Where, where but here have Pride and Truth,
That long to give themselves for wage,
To shake their wicked sides at youth
Restraining reckless middle-age.

TO A POET, WHO WOULD HAVE ME PRAISE CERTAIN BAD POETS, IMITATORS OF HIS AND MINE

You say, as I have often given tongue
In praise of what another's said or sung,
'Twere politic to do the like by these;
But where's the wild dog that has praised his fleas?

A LYRIC FROM
AN UNPUBLISHED PLAY

"Put off that mask of burning gold
With emerald eyes."
"O no, my dear, you make so bold
To find if hearts be wild and wise,
And yet not cold."

"I would but find what's there to find,
Love or deceit."
"It was the mask engaged your mind,
And after set your heart to beat,
Not what's behind."

"But lest you are my enemy,
I must enquire."
"O no, my dear, let all that be,
What matter, so there is but fire
In you, in me?"

UPON A HOUSE SHAKEN BY
THE LAND AGITATION

How should the world be luckier if this house,
Where passion and precision have been one
Time out of mind, became too ruinous
To breed the lidless eye that loves the sun?
And the sweet laughing eagle thoughts that grow
Where wings have memory of wings, and all
That comes of the best knit to the best? Although
Mean roof-trees were the sturdier for its fall,
How should their luck run high enough to reach
The gifts that govern men, and after these
To gradual Time's last gift, a written speech
Wrought of high laughter, loveliness and ease?

AT THE ABBEY THEATRE

(Imitated from Ronsard)

Dear Craoibhin Aoibhin, look into our case.
When we are high and airy hundreds say
That if we hold that flight they'll leave the place,
While those same hundreds mock another day
Because we have made our art of common things,
So bitterly, you'd dream they longed to look
All their lives through into some drift of wings.
You've dandled them and fed them from the book
And know them to the bone; impart to us—
We'll keep the secret—a new trick to please.
Is there a bridle for this Proteus
That turns and changes like his draughty seas?
Or is there none, most popular of men,
But when they mock us that we mock again?

THESE ARE THE CLOUDS

These are the clouds about the fallen sun,
The majesty that shuts his burning eye;
The weak lay hand on what the strong has done,
Till that be tumbled that was lifted high
And discord follow upon unison,
And all things at one common level lie.
And therefore, friend, if your great race were run
And these things came, so much the more thereby
Have you made greatness your companion,
Although it be for children that you sigh:
These are the clouds about the fallen sun,
The majesty that shuts his burning eye.

AT GALWAY RACES

Out yonder, where the race course is,
Delight makes all of the one mind,
Riders upon the swift horses,
The field that closes in behind:
We, too, had good attendance once,
Hearers and hearteners of the work;
Aye, horsemen for companions,
Before the merchant and the clerk
Breathed on the world with timid breath.
Sing on: sometime, and at some new moon,
We'll learn that sleeping is not death,
Hearing the whole earth change its tune,
Its flesh being wild, and it again
Crying aloud as the race course is,
And we find hearteners among men
That ride upon horses.

A FRIEND'S ILLNESS

Sickness brought me this
Thought, in that scale of his:
Why should I be dismayed
Though flame had burned the whole
World, as it were a coal,
Now I have seen it weighed
Against a soul?

ALL THINGS CAN TEMPT ME

All things can tempt me from this craft of verse:
One time it was a woman's face, or worse—
The seeming needs of my fool-driven land;
Now nothing but comes readier to the hand
Than this accustomed toil. When I was young,
I had not given a penny for a song
Did not the poet sing it with such airs
That one believed he had a sword upstairs;
Yet would be now, could I but have my wish,
Colder and dumber and deafer than a fish.

THE YOUNG MAN'S SONG

I whispered, "I am too young,"
And then, "I am old enough";
Wherefore I threw a penny
To find out if I might love;
"Go and love, go and love, young man,
If the lady be young and fair."
Ah, penny, brown penny, brown penny,
I am looped in the loops of her hair.

Oh love is the crooked thing,
There is nobody wise enough
To find out all that is in it,
For he would be thinking of love
Till the stars had run away,
And the shadows eaten the moon;
Ah, penny, brown penny, brown penny.
One cannot begin it too soon.

Responsibilities

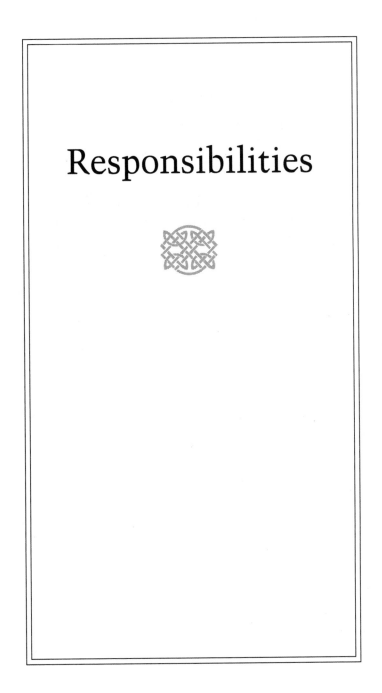

"*In dreams begins responsibility.*"

OLD PLAY

"*How am I fallen from myself, for a long time now I have not seen the Prince of Chang in my dreams.*"

KHOUNG-FOU-TSEU

Pardon, old fathers, if you still remain
Somewhere in earshot for the story's end,
Old Dublin merchant 'free of the ten and four'
Or trading out of Galway into Spain;
And country scholar, Robert Emmet's friend,
A hundred-year-old memory to the poor;
Merchant and scholar who have left me blood
That has not passed through any huckster's loin,
Soldiers that gave, whatever die was cast:
Old Butlers when you took to horse and stood
Beside the brackish waters of the Boyne
James and his Irish when the Dutchman crossed;
You merchant skipper that leaped overboard
After a ragged hat in Biscay Bay,
You most of all, silent and fierce old man,
Because you were the spectacle that stirred
My fancy, and set my boyish lips to say
"Only the wasteful virtues earn the sun";
Pardon that for a barren passion's sake,
Although I have come close on forty-nine
I have no child, I have nothing but a book,
Nothing to prove your blood and mine.

JANUARY *1914*

THE GREY ROCK

Poets with whom I learned my trade,
Companions of the Cheshire Cheese,
Here's an old story I've re-made,
Imaginging 'twould better please
Your ears than stories now in fashion,
Though you may think I waste my breath
Pretending that there can be passion
That has more life in it than death,
And though at bottling of your wine
The bow-legged Goban had no say;
The moral's yours because it's mine.

When cups went round at close of day—
Is not that how good stories run?—
Somewhere within some hollow hill,
If books speak truth in Slievenamon,
But let that be, the gods were still
And sleepy, having had their meal,
And smoky torches made a glare
On painted pillars, on a deal
Of fiddles and of flutes hung there
By the ancient holy hands that brought them
From murmuring Murias, on cups—
Old Goban hammered them and wrought them,
And put his pattern round their tops
To hold the wine they buy of him.
But from the juice that made them wise
All those had lifted up the dim
Imaginations of their eyes,
For one that was like woman made
Before their sleepy eyelids ran
And trembling with her passion said,

"Come out and dig for a dead man,
Who's burrowing somewhere in the ground,
And mock him to his face and then
Hollo him on with horse and hound,
For he is the worst of all dead men."

We should be dazed and terror struck,
If we but saw in dreams that room,
Those wine-drenched eyes, and curse our luck
That emptied all our days to come.
I knew a woman none could please,
Because she dreamed when but a child
Of men and women made like these;
And after, when her blood ran wild,
Had ravelled her own story out,
And said, "In two or in three years
I need must marry some poor lout,"
And having said it burst in tears.
Since, tavern comrades, you have died,
Maybe your images have stood,
Mere bone and muscle thrown aside,
Before that roomful or as good.
You had to face your ends when young—
'Twas wine or women, or some curse—
But never made a poorer song
That you might have a heavier purse,
Nor gave loud service to a cause
That you might have a troop of friends.
You kept the Muses' sterner laws,
And unrepenting faced your ends,
And therefore earned the right—and yet
Dowson and Johnson most I praise—
To troop with those the world's forgot,
And copy their proud steady gaze.

"The Danish troop was driven out
Between the dawn and dusk," she said;
"Although the event was long in doubt,
Although the King of Ireland's dead
And half the kings, before sundown
All was accomplished."

                              "When this day
Murrough, the King of Ireland's son,
Foot after foot was giving way,
He and his best troops back to back
Had perished there, but the Danes ran,
Stricken with panic from the attack,
The shouting of an unseen man;
And being thankful Murrough found,
Led by a footsole dipped in blood
That had made prints upon the ground,
Where by old thorn trees that man stood;
And though when he gazed here and there,
He had but gazed on thorn trees, spoke,
'Who is the friend that seems but air
And yet could give so fine a stroke?'
Thereon a young man met his eye,
Who said, 'Because she held me in
Her love, and would not have me die,
Rock-nurtured Aoife took a pin,
And pushing it into my shirt,
Promised that for a pin's sake,
No man should see to do me hurt;
But there it's gone; I will not take
The fortune that had been my shame
Seeing, King's son, what wounds you have.'
'Twas roundly spoke, but when night came
He had betrayed me to his grave,
For he and the King's son were dead.
I'd promised him two hundred years,

And when for all I'd done or said—
And these immortal eyes shed tears—
He claimed his country's need was most,
I'd save his life, yet for the sake
Of a new friend he has turned a ghost.
What does he care if my heart break?
I call for spade and horse and hound
That we may harry him." Thereon
She cast herself upon the ground
And rent her clothes and made her moan:
"Why are they faithless when their might
Is from the holy shades that rove
The grey rock and the windy light?
Why should the faithfullest heart most love
The bitter sweetness of false faces?
Why must the lasting love what passes,
Why are the gods by men betrayed!"

But thereon every god stood up
With a slow smile and without sound,
And stretching forth his arm and cup
To where she moaned upon the ground,
Suddenly drenched her to the skin;
And she with Goban's wine adrip,
No more remembering what had been,
       ed at the gods with laughing lip.

I have kept my faith, though faith was tried,
To that rock-born, rock-wandering foot,
And the world's altered since you died,
And I am in no good repute
With the loud host before the sea,
That think sword strokes were better meant
Than lover's music—let that be,
So that the wandering foot's content.

THE TWO KINGS

KING EOCHAID came at sundown to a wood
Westward of Tara. Hurrying to his queen
He had out-ridden his war-wasted men
That with empounded cattle trod the mire;
And where beech trees had mixed a pale green light
With the ground-ivy's blue, he saw a stag
Whiter than curds, its eyes the tint of the sea.
Because it stood upon his path and seemed
More hands in height than any stag in the world
He sat with tightened rein and loosened mouth
Upon his trembling horse, then drove the spur;
But the stag stooped and ran at him, and passed,
Rending the horse's flank. King Eochaid reeled
Then drew his sword to hold its levelled point
Against the stag. When horn and steel were met
The horn resounded as though it had been silver,
A sweet, miraculous, terrifying sound.
Horn locked in sword, they tugged and struggled there
As though a stag and unicorn were met
In Africa on Mountain of the Moon,
Until at last the double horns, drawn backward,
Butted below the single and so pierced
The entrails of the horse. Dropping his sword
King Eochaid seized the horns in his strong hands
And stared into the sea-green eye, and so
Hither and thither to and fro they trod
Till all the place was beaten into mire.
The strong thigh and the agile thigh were met,
The hands that gathered up the might of the world,
And hoof and horn that had sucked in their speed
Amid the elaborate wilderness of the air.
Through bush they plunged and over ivied root,

And where the stone struck fire, while in the leaves
A squirrel whinnied and a bird screamed out;
But when at last he forced those sinewy flanks
Against a beech bole, he threw down the beast
And knelt above it with drawn knife.
      On the instant
It vanished like a shadow, and a cry
So mournful that it seemed the cry of one
Who had lost some unimaginable treasure
Wandered between the blue and the green leaf
And climbed into the air, crumbling away,
Till all had seemed a shadow or a vision
But for the trodden mire, the pool of blood,
The disembowelled horse.
                King Eochaid ran,
Toward peopled Tara, nor stood to draw his breath
Until he came before the painted wall,
The posts of polished yew, circled with bronze,
Of the great door; but though the hanging lamps
Showed their faint light through the unshuttered windows,
Nor door, nor mouth, nor slipper made a noise,
Nor on the ancient beaten paths, that wound
From well-side or from plough-land, was there noise;
And there had been no sound of living thing
Before him or behind, but that far-off
On the horizon edge bellowed the herds.
Knowing that silence brings no good to kings,
And mocks returning victory, he passed
Between the pillars with a beating heart
And saw where in the midst of the great hall
Pale-faced, alone upon a bench, Edain
Sat upright with a sword before her feet.
Her hands on either side had gripped the bench,
Her eyes were cold and steady, her lips tight.
Some passion had made her stone. Hearing a foot
She started and then knew whose foot it was;

But when he thought to take her in his arms
She motioned him afar, and rose and spoke:
"I have sent among the fields or to the woods
The fighting men and servants of this house,
For I would have your judgment upon one
Who is self-accused. If she be innocent
She would not look in any known man's face
Till judgment has been given, and if guilty,
Will never look again on known man's face."
And at these words he paled, as she had paled,
Knowing that he should find upon her lips
The meaning of that monstrous day.
                                        Then she:
"You brought me where your brother Ardan sat
Always in his one seat, and bid me care him
Through that strange illness that had fixed him there,
And should he die to heap his burial mound
And carve his name in Ogham."
        Eochaid said,
"He lives?" "He lives and is a healthy man."
"While I have him and you it matters little
What man you have lost, what evil you have found."
"I bid them make his bed under this roof
And carried him his food with my own hands,
And so the weeks passed by. But when I said
'What is this trouble?' he would answer nothing,
Though always at my words his trouble grew;
And I but asked the more, till he cried out,
Weary of many questions: 'There are things
That make the heart akin to the dumb stone.'
Then I replied: 'Although you hide a secret,
Hopeless and dear, or terrible to think on,
Speak it, that I may send through the wide world
For medicine.' Thereon he cried aloud:
'Day after day you question me, and I,
Because there is such a storm amid my thoughts

I shall be carried in the gust, command,
Forbid, beseech and waste my breath.'
    Then I,
'Although the thing that you have hid were evil,
The speaking of it could be no great wrong,
And evil must it be, if done 'twere worse
Than mound and stone that keep all virtue in,
And loosen on us dreams that waste our life,
Shadows and shows that can but turn the brain.'
But finding him still silent I stooped down
And whispering that none but he should hear,
Said: 'If a woman has put this on you,
My men, whether it please her or displease,
And though they have to cross the Loughlan waters
And take her in the middle of armed men,
Shall make her look upon her handiwork,
That she may quench the rick she has fired; and though
She may have worn silk clothes, or worn a crown,
She'll not be proud, knowing within her heart
That our sufficient portion of the world
Is that we give, although it be brief giving,
Happiness to children and to men.'
Then he, driven by his thought beyond his thought,
And speaking what he would not though he would,
Sighed: 'You, even you yourself, could work the cure!'
And at those words I rose and I went out
And for nine days he had food from other hands,
And for nine days my mind went whirling round
The one disastrous zodiac, muttering
That the immedicable mound's beyond
Our questioning, beyond our pity even.
But when nine days had gone I stood again
Before his chair and bending down my head
Told him, that when Orion rose, and all
The women of his household were asleep,
To go—for hope would give his limbs the power—

To an old empty woodman's house that's hidden
Close to a clump of beech trees in the wood
Westward of Tara, there to await a friend
That could, as he had told her, work his cure
And would be no harsh friend.
                              When night had deepened,
I groped my way through boughs, and over roots,
Till oak and hazel ceased and beech began,
And found the house, a sputtering torch within,
And stretched out sleeping on a pile of skins
Ardan, and though I called to him and tried
To shake him out of sleep, I could not rouse him.
I waited till the night was on the turn,
Then fearing that some labourer, on his way
To plough or pasture-land, might see me there,
Went out.
          Among the ivy-covered rocks,
As on the blue light of a sword, a man
Who had unnatural majesty, and eyes
Like the eyes of some great kite scouring the woods,
Stood on my path. Trembling from head to foot
I gazed at him like grouse upon a kite;
But with a voice that had unnatural music,
'A weary wooing and a long,' he said,
'Speaking of love through other lips and looking
Under the eyelids of another, for it was my craft
That put a passion in the sleeper there,
And when I had got my will and drawn you here,
Where I may speak to you alone, my craft
Sucked up the passion out of him again
And left mere sleep. He'll wake when the sun wakes,
Push out his vigorous limbs and rub his eyes,
And wonder what has ailed him these twelve months.'
I cowered back upon the wall in terror,
But that sweet-sounding voice ran on:
      'Woman,

I was your husband when you rode the air,
Danced in the whirling foam and in the dust,
In days you have not kept in memory,
Being betrayed into a cradle, and I come
That I may claim you as my wife again."
I was no longer terrified, his voice
Had half awakened some old memory,
Yet answered him: 'I am King Eochaid's wife
And with him have found every happiness
Women can find.' With a most masterful voice,
That made the body seem as it were a string
Under a bow, he cried: 'What happiness
Can lovers have that know their happiness
Must end at the dumb stone? But where we build
Our sudden palaces in the still air
Pleasure itself can bring no weariness,
Nor can time waste the cheek, nor is there foot
That has grown weary of the whirling dance,
Nor an unlaughing mouth, but mine that mourns,
Among those mouths that sing their sweethearts' praise,
Your empty bed.' 'How should I love,' I answered,
'Were it not that when the dawn has lit my bed
And shown my husband sleeping there, I have sighed,
'Your strength and nobleness will pass away.'
Or how should love be worth its pains were it not
That when he has fallen asleep within my arms,
Being wearied out, I love in man the child?
What can they know of love that do not know
She builds her nest upon a narrow ledge
Above a windy precipice?' Then he:
'Seeing that when you come to the death-bed
You must return, whether you would or no,
This human life blotted from memory,
Why must I live some thirty, forty years,
Alone with all this useless happiness?'

Thereon he seized me in his arms, but I
Thrust him away with both my hands and cried,
'Never will I believe there is any change
Can blot out of my memory this life
Sweetened by death, but if I could believe
That were a double hunger in my lips
For what is doubly brief.'
                              And now the shape,
My hands were pressed to, vanished suddenly.
I staggered, but a beech tree stayed my fall,
And clinging to it I could hear the cocks
Crow upon Tara."
                              King Eochaid bowed his head
And thanked her for her kindness to his brother,
For that she promised, and for that refused.
Thereon the bellowing of the empounded herds
Rose round the walls, and through the bronze-ringed
        door
Jostled and shouted those war-wasted men,
And in the midst King Eochaid's brother stood.
He'd heard that din on the horizon's edge
And ridden towards it, being ignorant.

TO A FRIEND WHOSE WORK
HAS COME TO NOTHING

Now all the truth is out,
Be secret and take defeat
From any brazen throat,
For how can you compete,
Being honour bred, with one
Who, were it proved he lies,
Were neither shamed in his own
Nor in his neighbours' eyes?
Bred to a harder thing
Than Triumph, turn away
And like a laughing string
Whereon mad fingers play
Amid a place of stone,
Be secret and exult,
Because of all things known
That is most difficult.

TO A WEALTHY MAN WHO
PROMISED A SECOND SUBSCRIPTION
TO THE DUBLIN MUNICIPAL GALLERY
IF IT WERE PROVED
THE PEOPLE WANTED PICTURES

You gave but will not give again
Until enough of Paudeen's pence
By Biddy's halfpennies have lain
To be "some sort of evidence,"
Before you'll put your guineas down,
That things it were a pride to give
Are what the blind and ignorant town
Imagines best to make it thrive.
What cared Duke Ercole, that bid
His mummers to the market place,
What th' onion-sellers thought or did
So that his Plautus set the pace
For the Italian comedies?
And Guidobaldo, when he made
That grammar school of courtesies
Where wit and beauty learned their trade
Upon Urbino's windy hill,
Had sent no runners to and fro
That he might learn the shepherds' will.
And when they drove out Cosimo,
Indifferent how the rancour ran,
He gave the hours they had set free

To Michelozzo's latest plan
For the San Marco Library,
Whence turbulent Italy should draw
Delight in Art whose end is peace,
In logic and in natural law
By sucking at the dugs of Greece.
Your open hand but shows our loss,
For he knew better how to live.
Let Paudeens play at pitch and toss,
Look up in the sun's eye and give
What the exultant heart calls good
That some new day may breed the best
Because you gave, not what they would
But the right twigs for an eagle's nest!

December 1912

SEPTEMBER 1913

What need you, being come to sense,
But fumble in a greasy till
And add the halfpence to the pence
And prayer to shivering prayer, until
You have dried the marrow from the bor
For men were born to pray and save:
Romantic Ireland's dead and gone,
It's with O'Leary in the grave.

Yet they were of a different kind
The names that stilled your childish pla
They have gone about the world like w
But little time had they to pray
For whom the hangman's rope was sp
And what, God help us, could they sa
Romantic Ireland's dead and gone,
It's with O'Leary in the grave.

Was it for this the wild geese spread
The grey wing upon every tide;
For this that all that blood was shed,
For this Edward Fitzgerald died,
And Robert Emmet and Wolfe Tone
And all that delirium of the brave;
Romantic Ireland's dead and gone,
It's with O'Leary in the grave.

Yet could we turn the years again,
And call those exiles as they were,
In all their loneliness and pain
You'd cry "Some woman's yellow l
Has maddened every mother's son
They weighed so lightly what the
But let them be, they're dead and
They're with O'Leary in the grav

PAUDEEN

Indignant at the fumbling wits, the obscure spite
Of our old Paudeen in his shop, I stumbled blind
Among the stones and thorn trees, under morning light;
Until a curlew cried and in the luminous wind
A curlew answered; and suddenly thereupon I thought
That on the lonely height where all are in God's eye,
There cannot be, confusion of our sound forgot,
A single soul that lacks a sweet crystaline cry.

TO A SHADE

If you have revisited the town, thin Shade,
Whether to look upon your monument
(I wonder if the builder has been paid)
Or happier thoughted when the day is spent
To drink of that salt breath out of the sea
When grey gulls flit about instead of men,
And the gaunt houses put on majesty:
Let these content you and be gone again;
For they are at their old tricks yet.

                                    A man
Of your own passionate serving kind who had brought
In his full hands what, had they only known,
Had given their children's children loftier thought,
Sweeter emotion, working in their veins
Like gentle blood, has been driven from the place,
And insult heaped upon him for his pains
And for his open-handedness, disgrace;
An old foul mouth that slandered you had set
The pack upon him.

                        Go, unquiet wanderer,
And gather the Glasnevin coverlet
About your head till the dust stops your ear,
The time for you to taste of that salt breath
And listen at the corners has not come;
You had enough of sorrow before death—
Away, away! You are safer in the tomb.

SEPTEMBER 29TH, 1914

WHEN HELEN LIVED

We have cried in our despair
That men desert,
For some trivial affair
Or noisy, insolent sport,
Beauty that we have won
From bitterest hours;
Yet we, had we walked within
Those topless towers
Where Helen walked with her boy,
Had given but as the rest
Of the men and women of Troy,
A word and a jest.

THE ATTACK ON
"THE PLAYBOY OF THE
WESTERN WORLD," 1907

Once, when midnight smote the air,
Eunuchs ran through Hell and met
From thoroughfare to thoroughfare,
While that great Juan galloped by;
And like these to rail and sweat
Staring upon his sinewy thigh.

THE THREE BEGGARS

"Though to my feathers in the wet,
I have stood here from break of day,
I have not found a thing to eat
For only rubbish comes my way.
Am I to live on lebeen-lone?"
Muttered the old crane of Gort.
"For all my pains on lebeen-lone."

King Guari walked amid his court
The palace-yard and river-side
And there to three old beggars said:
"You that have wandered far and wide
Can ravel out what's in my head.
Do men who least desire get most,
Or get the most who most desire?"
A beggar said: "They get the most
Whom man or devil cannot tire,
And what could make their muscles taut
Unless desire had made them so."
But Guari laughed with secret thought,
"If that be true as it seems true,
One of you three is a rich man,
For he shall have a thousand pounds
Who is first asleep, if but he can
Sleep before the third noon sounds."
And thereon merry as a bird,
With his old thoughts King Guari went
From river-side and palace-yard
And left them to their argument.
"And if I win," one beggar said,
"Though I am old I shall persuade
A pretty girl to share my bed";

The second: "I shall learn a trade";
The third: "I'll hurry to the course
Among the other gentlemen,
And lay it all upon a horse";
The second: "I have thought again:
A farmer has more dignity."
One to another sighed and cried:
The exorbitant dreams of beggary,
That idleness had borne to pride,
Sang through their teeth from noon to noon;
And when the second twilight brought
The frenzy of the beggars' moon
They closed their blood-shot eyes for naught.
One beggar cried: "You're shamming sleep."
And thereupon their anger grew
Till they were whirling in a heap.

They'd mauled and bitten the night through
Or sat upon their heels to rail,
And when old Guari came and stood
Before the three to end this tale,
They were commingling lice and blood.
"Time's up," he cried, and all the three
With blood-shot eyes upon him stared.
"Time's up," he cried, and all the three
Fell down upon the dust and snored.

"Maybe I shall be lucky yet,
Now they are silent," said the crane.
"Though to my feathers in the wet
I've stood as I were made of stone
And seen the rubbish run about,
It's certain there are trout somewhere
And maybe I shall take a trout
If but I do not seem to care."

THE THREE HERMITS

Three old hermits took the air
By a cold and desolate sea,
First was muttering a prayer,
Second rummaged for a flea;
On a windy stone, the third,
Giddy with his hundredth year,
Sang unnoticed like a bird.
"Through the Door of Death is near
And what waits behind the door,
Three times in a single day
I, though upright on the shore,
Fall asleep when I should pray."
So the first but now the second,
"We're but given what we have earned
When all thoughts and deeds are reckoned,
So it's plain to be discerned
That the shades of holy men,
Who have failed being weak of will,
Pass the Door of Birth again,
And are plagued by crowds, until
They've the passion to escape."
Moaned the other, "They are thrown
Into some most fearful shape."
But the second mocked his moan:
"They are not changed to anything,
Having loved God once, but maybe,
To a poet or a king
Or a witty lovely lady."
While he'd rummaged rags and hair,
Caught and cracked his flea, the third,
Giddy with his hundredth year
Sang unnoticed like a bird.

BEGGAR TO BEGGAR CRIED

"Time to put off the world and go somewhere
And find my health again in the sea air,"
Beggar to beggar cried, being frenzy-struck,
"And make my soul before my pate is bare."

"And get a comfortable wife and house
To rid me of the devil in my shoes,"
Beggar to beggar cried, being frenzy-struck,
"And the worse devil that is between my thighs."

"And though I'd marry with a comely lass,
She need not be too comely—let it pass,"
Beggar to beggar cried, being frenzy-struck,
"But there's a devil in a looking-glass."

"Nor should she be too rich, because the rich
Are driven by wealth as beggars by the itch,"
Beggar to beggar cried, being frenzy-struck,
"And cannot have a humorous happy speech."

"And there I'll grow respected at my ease,
And hear amid the garden's nightly peace,"
Beggar to beggar cried, being frenzy-struck,
"The wind-blown clamor of the barnacle-geese."

THE WELL AND THE TREE

"The Man that I praise,"
Cries out the empty well,
"Lives all his days
Where a hand on the bell
Can call the milch-cows
To the comfortable door of his house.
Who but an idiot would praise
Dry stones in a well?"

"The Man that I praise,"
Cries out the leafless tree,
"Has married and stays
By an old hearth, and he
On naught has set store
But children and dogs on the floor.
Who but an idiot would praise
A withered tree?"

RUNNING TO PARADIS

As I came over Windy Gap
They threw a halfpenny into my cap,
For I am running to Paradise;
And all that I need do is to wish
And somebody puts his hand in the dish
To throw me a bit of salted fish:
And there the king *is* but as the beggar.

My brother Mourteen is worn out
With skelping his big brawling lout,
And I am running to Paradise;
A poor life do what he can,
And though he keep a dog and a gun,
A serving maid and a serving man:
And there the king *is* but as the beggar.

Poor men have grown to be rich men,
And rich men grown to be poor again,
And I am running to Paradise;
And many a darling wit's grown dull
That tossed a bare heel when at school,
Now it has filled an old sock full:
And there the king *is* but as the beggar.

The wind is old and still at play
While I must hurry upon my way,
For I am running to Paradise;
Yet never have I lit on a friend
To take my fancy like the wind
That nobody can buy or bind:
And there the king *is* but as the beggar.

THE HOUR BEFORE DAWN

A one-legged, one-armed, one-eyed man,
A bundle of rags upon a crutch,
Stumbled on windy Cruachan
Cursing the wind. It was as much
As the one sturdy leg could do
To keep him upright while he cursed.
He had counted, where long years ago
Queen Maeve's nine Maines had been nursed,
A pair of lapwings, one old sheep
And not a house to the plain's edge,
When close to his right hand a heap
Of grey stones and a rocky ledge
Reminded him that he could make,
If he but shifted a few stones,
A shelter till the daylight broke.
But while he fumbled with the stones
They toppled over; "Were it not
I have a lucky wooden shin
I had been hurt"; and toppling brought
Before his eyes, where stones had been,
A dark deep hole in the rock's face.
He gave a gasp and thought to run,
Being certain it was no right place
But the Hell Mouth at Cruachan
That's stuffed with all that's old and bad,
And yet stood still, because inside
He had seen a red-haired jolly lad
In some outlandish coat beside
A ladle and a tub of beer,
Plainly no phantom by his look.
So with a laugh at his own fear
He crawled into that pleasant nook.

Young Red-head stretched himself to yawn
And murmured, "May God curse the night
That's grown uneasy near the dawn
So that it seems even I sleep light;
And who are you that wakens me?
Has one of Maeve's nine brawling sons
Grown tired of his own company?
But let him keep his grave for once
I have to find the sleep I have lost."
And then at last being wide awake,
"I took you for a brawling ghost,
Say what you please, but from daybreak
I'll sleep another century."
The beggar deaf to all but hope
Went down upon a hand and knee
And took the wooden ladle up
And would have dipped it in the beer
But the other pushed his hand aside,
"Before you have dipped it in the beer
That sacred Goban brewed," he cried,
"I'd have assurance that you are able
To value beer—I will have no fool
Dipping his nose into my ladle
Because he has stumbled on this hole
In the bad hour before the dawn.
If you but drink that beer and say
I will sleep until the winter's gone,
Or maybe, to Midsummer Day
You will sleep that length; and at the first
I waited so for that or this—
Because the weather was a-cursed
Or I had no woman there to kiss,
And slept for half a year or so;
But year by year I found that less
Gave me such pleasure I'd forgo
Even a half hour's nothingness,

And when at one year's end I found
I had not waked a single minute,
I chose this burrow under ground
I will sleep away all Time within it:
My sleep were now nine centuries
But for those mornings when I find
The lapwing at their foolish cries
And the sheep bleating at the wind
As when I also played the fool."
The beggar in a rage began
Upon his hunkers in the hole,
"It's plain that you are no right man
To mock at everything I love
As if it were not worth the doing.
I'd have a merry life enough
If a good Easter wind were blowing,
And though the winter wind is bad
I should not be too down in the mouth
For anything you did or said
If but this wind were in the south."
But the other cried, "You long for spring
Or that the wind would shift a point
And do not know that you would bring,
If time were suppler in the joint,
Neither the spring nor the south wind
But the hour when you shall pass away
And leave no smoking wick behind,
For all life longs for the Last Day
And there's no man but cocks his ear
To know when Michael's trumpet cries
That flesh and bone may disappear,
And souls as if they were but sighs,
And there be nothing but God left;
But I alone being blessed keep
Like some old rabbit to my cleft
And wait Him in a drunken sleep."

He dipped his ladle in the tub
And drank and yawned and stretched him out.
The other shouted, "You would rob
My life of every pleasant thought
And every comfortable thing
And so take that and that." Thereon
He gave him a great pummelling,
But might have pummelled at a stone
For all the sleeper knew or cared;
And after heaped the stones again
And cursed and prayed, and prayed and cursed:
"Oh God if he got loose!" And then
In fury and in panic fled
From the Hell Mouth at Cruachan
And gave God thanks that overhead
The clouds were brightening with the dawn.

THE PLAYER QUEEN

(Song from an Unfinished Play)

My mother dandled me and sang,
"How young it is, how young!"
And made a golden cradle
That on a willow swung.

"He went away," my mother sang,
"When I was brought to bed,"
And all the while her needle pulled
The gold and silver thread.

She pulled the thread and bit the
    thread
And made a golden gown,
And wept because she had dreamt that I
Was born to wear a crown.

"When she was got," my mother sang,
"I heard a sea-mew cry,
And saw a flake of the yellow foam
That dropped upon my thigh."

How therefore could she help but
    braid
The gold into my hair,
And dream that I should carry
The golden top of care?

THE REALISTS

Hope that you may understand!
What can books of men that wive
In a dragon-guarded land,
Paintings of the dolphin-drawn
Sea-nymphs in their pearly waggons
Do, but awake a hope to live
That had gone
With the dragons?

I

THE WITCH

Toil and grow rich,
What's that but to lie
With a foul witch
And after, drained dry,
To be brought
To the chamber where
Lies one long sought
With despair.

II

THE PEACOCK

What's riches to him
That has made a great peacock
With the pride of his eye?
The wind-beaten, stone-grey,
And desolate Three-rock
Would nourish his whim.
Live he or die
Amid wet rocks and heather,
His ghost will be gay
Adding feather to feather
For the pride of his eye.

THE MOUNTAIN TOMB

Pour wine and dance if Manhood still have pride,
Bring roses if the rose be yet in bloom;
The cataract smokes upon the mountain side,
Our Father Rosicross is in his tomb.

Pull down the blinds, bring fiddle and clarionet
That there be no foot silent in the room
Nor mouth from kissing, nor from wine unwet;
Our Father Rosicross is in his tomb.

In vain, in vain; the cataract still cries
The everlasting taper lights the gloom;
All wisdom shut into his onyx eyes
Our Father Rosicross sleeps in his tomb.

TO A CHILD DANCING
IN THE WIND

I

Dance there upon the shore;
What need have you to care
For wind or water's roar?
And tumble out your hair
That the salt drops have wet;
Being young you have not known
The fool's triumph, nor yet
Love lost as soon as won,
Nor the best labourer dead
And all the sheaves to bind.
What need have you to dread
The monstrous crying of wind?

II

Has no one said those daring
Kind eyes should be more learn'd?
Or warned you how despairing
The moths are when they are burned,
I could have warned you, but you are
        young,
So we speak a different tongue.

O you will take whatever's offered
And dream that all the world's a
        friend,
Suffer as your mother suffered,
Be as broken in the end.
But I am old and you are young,
And I speak a barbarous tongue.

A MEMORY OF YOUTH

The moments passed as at a play,
I had the wisdom love brings forth;
I had my share of mother wit
And yet for all that I could say,
And though I had her praise for it,
A cloud blown from the cut-throat
    north
Suddenly hid love's moon away.

Believing every word I said
I praised her body and her mind
Till pride had made her eyes grow
    bright,
And pleasure made her cheeks grow
    red,
And vanity her footfall light,
Yet we, for all that praise, could find
Nothing but darkness overhead.
We sat as silent as a stone,
We knew, though she'd not said a
    word,
That even the best of love must die,
And had been savagely undone
Were it not that love upon the cry
Of a most ridiculous little bird
Tore from the clouds his marvellous
    moon.

FALLEN MAJESTY

Although crowds gathered once if
    she but showed her face,
And even old men's eyes grew dim,
    this hand alone,
Like some last courtier at a gypsy
    camping place,
Babbling of fallen majesty, records
    what's gone.

The lineaments, a heart that laughter
    has made sweet,
These, these remain, but I record
    what's gone. A crowd
Will gather, and not know it walks
    the very street
Whereon a thing once walked that
    seemed a burning cloud.

FRIENDS

Now must I these three praise—
Three women that have wrought
What joy is in my days;
One that no passing thought,
Nor those unpassing cares,
No, not in these fifteen
Many times troubled years,
Could ever come between
Heart and delighted heart;
And one because her hand
Had strength that could unbind
What none can understand,
What none can have and thrive,
Youth's dreamy load, till she
So changed me that I live
Labouring in ecstasy.
And what of her that took
All till my youth was gone
With scarce a pitying look?
How should I praise that one?
When day begins to break
I count my good and bad,
Being wakeful for her sake,
Remembering what she had,
What eagle look still shows,
While up from my heart's root
So great a sweetness flows
I shake from head to foot.

THE COLD HEAVEN

Suddenly I saw the cold and rook delighting Heaven
That seemed as though ice burned and was but the
      more ice,
And thereupon imagination and heart were driven
So wild, that every casual thought of that and this
Vanished, and left but memories, that should be out of
      season
With the hot blood of youth, of love crossed long ago;
And I took all the blame out of all sense and reason,
Until I cried and trembled and rocked to and fro,
Riddled with light. Ah! when the ghost begins to
      quicken,
Confusion of the death-bed over, is it sent
Out naked on the roads, as the books say, and stricken
By the injustice of the skies for punishment?

THAT THE NIGHT COME

She lived in storm and strife.
Her soul had such desire
For what proud death may bring
That it could not endure
The common good of life,
But lived as 't were a king
That packed his marriage day
With banneret and pennon,
Trumpet and kettledrum,
And the outrageous cannon,
To bundle Time away
That the night come.

AN APPOINTMENT

Being out of heart with government
I took a broken root to fling
Where the proud, wayward squirrel went,
Taking delight that he could spring;
And he, with that low whinnying sound
That is like laughter, sprang again
And so to the other tree at a bound.
Nor the tame will, nor timid brain,
Nor heavy knitting of the brow
Bred that fierce tooth and cleanly limb
And threw him up to laugh on the bough;
No government appointed him.

THE MAGI

Now as at all times I can see in the mind's eye,
In their stiff, painted clothes the pale unsatisfied ones
Appear and disappear in the blue depth of the sky
With all their ancient faces like rain-beaten stones,
And all their helms of silver hovering side by side,
And all their eyes still fixed, hoping to find once more,
Being by Calvary's turbulence unsatisfied,
The uncontrollable mystery on the bestial floor.

THE DOLLS

A doll in the doll-maker's house
Looks at the cradle and bawls:
"That is an insult to us."
But the oldest of all the dolls
Who had seen, being kept for show,
Generations of his sort,
Out-screams the whole shelf: "Although
There's not a man can report
Evil of this place,
The man and the woman bring
Hither to our disgrace,
A noisy and filthy thing."
Hearing him groan and stretch
The doll-maker's wife is aware
Her husband has heard the wretch,
And crouched by the arm of his chair,
She murmurs into his ear,
Head upon shoulder leant:
"My dear, my dear, oh dear,
It was an accident."

A COAT

I made my song a coat
Covered with embroideries
Out of old mythologies
From heel to throat;
But the fools caught it,
Wore it in the world's eye
As though they'd wrought it.
Song, let them take it
For there's more enterprise
In walking naked.

While I, from that reed-throated whisperer
Who comes at need, although not now as once
A clear articulation in the air
But inwardly, surmise companions
Beyond the fling of the dull ass's hoof,
Ben Jonson's phrase—and find when June is come
At Kyle-na-no under that ancient roof
A sterner conscience and a friendlier home
I can forgive even that wrong of wrongs.
Those undreamt accidents that have made me
—Seeing that Fame has perished this long while
Being but a part of ancient ceremony—
Notorious, till all of priceless things
Are but a post the passing dogs defile.